TOWARD A NEW
POLITICS IN THE SOUTH

TOWARD A NEW POLITICS IN THE SOUTH

by

Jasper Berry Shannon

THE UNIVERSITY OF TENNESSEE PRESS
KNOXVILLE
1949

Copyright
by
The University of Tennessee Press
1949

FOREWORD

Jasper Berry Shannon, a native of Kentucky and presently Professor of Political Science at the University of Kentucky is especially well equipped by nature, by training, and by an active and varied career to speak on the subject of Southern politics. For that reason he was invited to become Visiting Professor at The University of Tennessee during the summer of 1947 and in that capacity delivered the series of lectures now published in this book. The lectures are printed here substantially as delivered; we have not attempted to bring them up to the present in all instances, for we believe Professor Shannon's principal points are not made invalid by events which have occurred since 1947. It is understood, of course, that Professor Shannon's point of view is his own; no one who understands educational institutions or their functions would expect those institutions to represent one particular outlook on most subjects, least of all, on politics. We are happy to have this opportunity to make these challenging essays available to a wider public.

Various members of the staff of the Bureau of Public Administration have aided in the preparation of the manuscript for printing. We wish also to thank the staff of the University Press for generous aid and counsel.

Lee S. Greene

CONTENTS

	PAGE
PARTY, TRADITION, AND REGION IN SOUTHERN POLITICS	1
VOTING IN THE SOUTH; PAST, PRESENT AND FUTURE	16
THE GOVERNING CLASS OF A SOUTHERN COUNTY SEAT	38
THE SOUTH AND THE FUTURE OF THE DEMOCRATIC PARTY	54
SOUTHERN POLITICS IN AN ATOMIC AGE; A CREATIVE FUTURE?	73

I

PARTY, TRADITION, AND REGION IN SOUTHERN POLITICS

*F*REE men have the opportunity to make choices. Party systems or institutions are the social growths which make possible the exercise of such choices. Both the conception of freedom and the development of party stem from the idea that man is rational, that is, capable of choosing between alternatives. In his blind grappling for freedom to dissent in religion, man searched for avenues of expression of heresy. In the seventeenth and eighteenth centuries this search in England was rewarded by a discovery that dissenting groups could form coalitions or parts of the whole which ultimately might become the "government." This growth, which Englishmen in characteristic fits of absence of mind failed to recognize for a century, is one of the greatest of all social inventions, as significant in the political world as the application of steam power to the process of production in the industrial world. For this new device made it possible to transfer political power from one governing class to another without the use of violence; it was, in a word, the evolutionary use of ballots rather than the revolutionary use of bullets.

Englishmen, transplanted to the American side of the Atlantic, not only observed the development of the party process at a distance but saw new adaptations of it on American soil. From Bacon's Rebellion in 1676 until the American Revolution itself there were repeated evidences of this new party process making itself felt. As a matter of fact the Revolution itself was in no small measure an effort to achieve an independence for the new parties of the new world and to win recognition of new coalitions of powers within each of the colonies. Finally, these groups formed themselves into factions for and against the policies of the Crown with the Committees of Correspondence furnishing the skeletons of party organization so vital to effective party action. In other words, parties exist to give living form to the dynamic political forces of an epoch. Politics, therefore, is the art, or science, if you please, of reconciliation and adjustment of intergroup and sometimes interpersonal conflicts.

Out of differences of religious points of view developed the Bill of Rights in the American constitution. From freedom of speech and of press, the recognition of diversity of belief, and the necessity of a majority for the choice of federal officials arose the political conditions essential to the existence of parties and probably of two parties only.[1] From the beginning of the federal government with Hamilton and Jefferson in Washington's cabinet there have been two divergent conceptions of what should be the American way of life. One of these points of view took a Physiocratic outlook on the future and foresaw an agrarian America, a commonwealth composed of farmers independent of industry and commerce or a society which fostered the "encouragement of agriculture, and of commerce as its handmaid," as Jefferson expressed it in his first inaugural address. The other school of thought, the Hamiltonian view, wished to see America commercial and industrial as well as agricultural or even predominantly industrial.

Where does the South fall within these broad outlines of social conflict? First of all, the tradition of the South is fundamentally feudal. The feudal view of life bases its chief values upon land and the relation of man to the soil. The feudal approach conceives of stability and permanence as of more value than change and flux. The feudal perspective regards status and hierarchy in themselves as desirable aspects of society and government. A feudal order is held together by an intermixture of loyalty and command, a recognition of the organic relation between leader and led.[2] It sees the nature of man as Aristotle saw it, diverse enough to make some men natural slaves and others natural masters. The natural slave is bound to his master, and by the ties of interest both are linked to the soil. As such, a slave is entitled to the rights of one of his kind as long as he performs the duties for which he is uniquely qualified. Since one man is destined by nature to be a slave he is failing in his purpose, the end for which he exists, when he attempts to be his own master. It is just as bad for the master to attempt to labor as for a slave to attempt to be a master. Both violate the laws of nature. Failure to abide by this natural law of difference would be destructive of man's chief purpose in life, to perform the distinctive function for which he was created.[3] Accordingly, a feudal order conceives of each man belonging to an hierarchical order of inequality in which his peculiar faculties equip him to perform a unique role in some part of the hierarchy. Equality of rights arises only from the performance of functionally necessary purposes.

Institutionally, the southern plantation was essentially the importation into the new world of the feudal manor. However, the abundance of free land made it difficult, if not impossible, to maintain a feudal system based on scarcity of land.[4] The introduction into the new world of a primitive non-European people to perform labor gave a somewhat different façade to the manor and the fact that the worker was bound to the master and not the soil added a slightly different color to the arrangement. The ethic was primarily the same. The traditional southern values became those of a feudal society. At the top of the hierarchy was a leisure class divorced from labor and free to develop a "culture" of philosophy, literature, and politics. In other words, the landed gentry became the governing class of the old South and the large estate or plantation the political center of gravity of the section. Let Henry Adams describe a member of this group in Harvard College during the 1850's.

Lee known through life as "Roony," was a Virginian of the eighteenth century, much as Henry Adams was a Bostonian of the same age. Roony Lee had changed little from the type of his grandfather, Light Horse Harry. Tall, largely built, handsome, genial, with liberal Virginian openness towards all he liked, he had also the Virginian habit of command and took leadership as his natural habit. . . . . The habit of command was not enough, and the Virginian had little else. He was simple beyond analysis; so simple that even the simple New England student could not realize him. No one knew enough to know how ignorant he was; how childlike; how helpless before the relative complexity of a school. As an animal, the Southerner seemed to have every advantage, but even as an animal he steadily lost ground.

. . . . Strictly, the Southerner had no mind; he had temperament. He was not a scholar; he had no intellectual training; he could not analyze an idea, and he could not even conceive of admitting two; but in life one could get along very well without ideas, if one had only the social instinct. Dozens of eminent statesmen were men of Lee's type, and maintained themselves well enough in the legislature, but college was a sharper test. The Virginian was weak in vice itself, though the Bostonian was hardly a master of crime. The habits of neither were good; both were apt to drink hard and to live low lives; but the Bostonian suffered less than the Virginian. Commonly the Bostonian would take some care of himself even in his worst stages, while the Virginian became quarrelsome and dangerous. When a Virginian had brooded a few days over an imaginary grief and substantial whiskey, none of his Northern friends could be sure that he might not be waiting, round the corner, with a knife or pistol, to revenge insult by the dry light of *delirium tremens*; and when things reached this condition, Lee had to exhaust his authority over his own staff. Lee was a gentleman of the old school, and, as every one knows, gentlemen of the old school drank almost as much as gentlemen of the new school; but this was not his trouble. He was sober even in the excessive violence of political feeling in those years; he kept his temper and his friends under control.[5]

This gentleman caste gave a distorted perspective to the whole of southern life. As Thorstein Veblen has so effectively pointed out in his *Theory of the Leisure Class*,[6] the values of the leisured elite, namely, conspicuous waste and invidious consumption, that is, the waste of labor and of soil as an evidence of hospitality, even of prodigality, became patterns of all southern society. Physical labor of any sort became an earmark of social inferiority, the badge of slavery. Accordingly, the son of the plantation owner and his idle slave or the careless "poor white trash" have in common the dislike of labor as a label or mark of social unworthiness.

On the other hand, the ownership or possession of slaves became a mark of distinction, and evidence of social prestige, a goal of social climbers. In this fashion, the landed gentry with their conception of politics and the army as worthy careers in contrast to business and industry, gave a belligerent tone to southern life in the strife for honorific achievement and at the same time set an overemphasis on oratory and statesmanship as evidences of belonging to a genuine governing class of gentlemen. As a careful student of southern culture has described it: "Money was seldom the object of these well-born gentlemen in accepting public office. The love of honor, the tradition of the family, and *noblesse oblige* were the dominant motives."[7]

The prevalence of the practice of dueling with its code of highly sensitized "honor" was another element in the ethic of the landed elite. The seclusion and extraordinarily developed refinements of females was a concomitant of an essentially feudal outlook—a stereotype still much in existence in the reluctance of southern females to be women rather than "ladies." A woman works; a lady is purely decorative, a nonutilitarian object of adoration. Of course, a lady must have servants. A proper appreciation of this cultural residue is necessary to a correct understanding of the unpopularity of Mrs. Eleanor Roosevelt in many feminine quarters in the South. This pattern of female inutility is a part of the mosaic of southern social traditions. It is part of the role of sex in the peculiar complex of southern problems which is at the heart of the political process, "the pictures in the heads" of southerners, if we may borrow the useful phrase of Mr. Walter Lippmann.[8]

This was not the only South. As Eaton observes,

> An aristocracy necessarily implies the existence of a large body of plebeians. The census of 1790 indicates that approximately two thirds of the white population of the South did not belong to slaveholding families. Nevertheless, this large body of commoners were prevented from playing a dominant role in politics by the property qualifications on voting, their lack of education, the difficulty of communication, and, above all, by their own attitude toward government. They were accustomed to follow aristocratic leadership. Consequently, it was the tradition for the leading families to provide the political representatives of the county and the state.[9]

In general we can call this the "Old South," the lowland South, the region of highly fertile, prevailingly phosphatic soils, rich enough to support an inefficient slave economy devoted to cotton, tobacco, sugar cane, rice, or hemp. But there was and is an upland or highland South—the South of the Appalachian hills, the sand hills, the piney woods, of the more rugged and the steeper slopes and infertile soils. Many of the earlier explorers pushed beyond the Tidewater, Black Belt, Delta, or Bluegrass into the surrounding hills. Life was not so easy, save here and there in a fertile bottom or occasional wide plain. This was pioneer life, based upon a marginal self-sustaining agriculture. Remote from waterway, or subsequently from rail and highways, this folk was bypassed by the rush of civilization. It retained the crude technology of wood and handicraft, the technologically wasteful labor of the hand.

No less proud or sensitive, frequently bringing the Scotch or Scotch-Irish Highlander's fierce independence from the old world, the mountaineer resented the lowlander's better manners as a "high hat" attitude but especially he rebelled against the lowlander's pretensions to an aristocratic ancestry which he rightly suspected went no further back than the same steerages that housed his own ancestors on their way to the new land. Most of all he disliked the usurpation of the best lands and along with them the right and power to govern.[10] The slave he hated as a badge of the inferiority of toil, an invidious reflection upon his own social status, for in his quest for the fertile valley soils opportunity was denied him by the legal title of the plantation owner and the servile labor of the black slave. Sometimes his social ambitions led him to emulate his wealthier valley neighbors and to acquire slaves for domestic labor in his home to release his wife, mother, or daughter from the onerous and socially degrading physical drudgery of home or farm. Out of this cleavage of geographically determined outlook grew the forces of difference, the nuclei for two parties prior to the War between the States.

The slaveholding and lowland dwelling elite formed the core of a group of Federalists of whom George Washington served as a symbol and prototype. Later under the aegis of the Whigs, Henry Clay, erstwhile Jeffersonian, but now a border state large landowner and extensive slaveholder, became the leader of the southern aristocracy. He symbolized by urbanity of demeanor and suavity of manners, the elegance of a Bluegrass elite which antagonized the hill farmers who preferred the soldier represented as a plain man of the people, Andrew Jackson, though the latter belonged to the Tennessee landed gentry no less than Clay did to Kentucky's. Visitors to the Hermitage can easily testify to the quality of Jackson's living, but he had better publicity agents both then among the journalists and now among the historians. In fact both belonged to a postfrontier squirearchy which loved good living, horse racing, drinking, gambling, and the usual leisure class type of living.[11]

To many historians, it is still a mystery how the landed gentry, though a minority of the population in the southern states, succeeded in persuading the great body of yeomen to follow them in the secession movement.[12] Only the strong ties of agriculture, a fierce local pride, the general acceptance by the farmers of the values of the slaveholders can explain secession in opposition to the real interests of the numerous small farmers. As it was, many of those small holders in Virginia, Alabama, Tennessee, Georgia, and North Carolina were loyal to the Union. The geologist Shaler speculates that if the limestone belt in Kentucky had run one hundred miles further north, secession would have succeeded, for Kentucky would have left the Union and given the South a defensible frontier, the Ohio River.[13] At any rate Lincoln commented that he wanted God on his side but he had to have Kentucky![14]

We have enough to indicate clearly the role of region and geography in the determination of the ante-bellum politics of the South. It is likewise clear that the two-party system is not foreign to the experience of the South, that the historic base for a two-party system has existed and continues to exist in geographic division between highlands and lowlands. It is our task to find out why the two-party system has failed to grow in the South in later years.

Like many of the issues of the contemporary South, the absence of a two-party system can be explained only by tracing its roots to the Reconstruction Era. It is well to remember that Abraham Lincoln and the newly formed Republican party did not have a majority of the popular vote in 1860. If the South had not made the tragic blunder of secession, the opponents of Lincoln would have been able to block for generations any efforts of Lincoln at emancipation or interference in the local affairs of southern states. Even the enactment of high tariff legislation, the establishment of national banks, and the provision for free distribution of government lands could have been defeated by the combination of farmers and workers formed by Jefferson and Jackson. The backbone of the Democratic party could have been maintained. In other words, Lincoln and Seward could not have put into effect the Hamilton-Clay program of industrial planning.

Likewise, the military triumph of the Union with the reincorporation of the southern states might have once more united the cotton and tobacco farmers with the wheat and corn-hog farmers of the West to give the Democrats control of the federal government. To avoid this possibility it seemed necessary to the so-called Radical Republicans, led by Sumner in the Senate and Stevens in the House, to enfranchise the newly emancipated Negroes and thereby give a solid block of Republican votes, to offset the returned Confederates if they could not be disfranchised completely.[15] The result of this policy is well known, and requires no elaboration at this point. Suffice it to say that reason flew out the window and violence in the form of the Ku Klux Klan took its place. Blind spots were formed, and the shibboleth of white supremacy was raised to haunt the politics of the South for generations to come. The details of the matter will be examined more minutely subsequently.

It was as an outgrowth of the bitter controversy over slavery and the proposed enfranchisement of the Negroes that the pattern of politics was frozen for the South. The two-party system came to an end, and the issues of the past rather than those of the present became the subject matter of political action. The Democratic party was the instrument employed by the new governing class to prevent a social revolution. Adherence to the name and symbol of Democracy became the chief article of faith in the new political creed. The issues of 1860–90, a social conflict which was resolved in part by bloodshed, became sealed in the forms of custom. Certain counties became Republican and certain ones Democratic. From that day to this these counties have voted the same way regardless of issues or candidates. Not only did the Democratic party become a closed corporation dedicated to the preservation of an outmoded way of life but the Republican party likewise, where it existed in the South, became embalmed in the memory of past conflicts. Its membership was hard, embittered, and inflexible, with little in common with the dominant big business industrial wing of the party. In certain areas one is born into the Democratic party and in others into the Republican party. Conceptions of public welfare or policy have nothing to do with one's membership in either party. One is born into the party as much as, or perhaps even more, than he is born within a church. To question one's loyalty to the party is to question one's patriotism, his religion, his faith. This freezing of party membership, this hardening of party issues on the basis of the past, tends to destroy effective democratic government and the free way of life. No longer does a citizen have an alternative, a choice between two courses of action, for party has become a tradition, a crust of custom so thick and heavy that no amount of reason can alter it.

It was under such circumstances of party crystallization that the long depression of agricultural prices following the Civil War hit the South. The control of the American economy by new forms of business enterprise, big business, if you will, through railway developments and corporate organization made well nigh impossible the recovery of southern agriculture. Under such circumstances the reunion of the South and West with northern and eastern organized labor was a natural development to be expected and it was attempted, unsuccessfully, first through the Populist party and, subsequently, in 1896 through Bryan and the Democratic party.[16] This struggle revealed clearly the fissures within the Democratic party notwithstanding the solid façade presented to the outside. It resulted in state constitutional action to prevent the juncture of emancipated slaves and hill farmers, the possible formation of a real majority party against the new governing class which had concentrated in the county seats the real political power of the Democratic party.

Eventually the struggle between the governing class and the poor farmers became so bitter that the convention system of nomination and selection of candidates had to be discarded. The primary system of choice of candidates rather rapidly replaced the convention method in all the southern states. In no small measure the primary was welcomed in the South because it did afford an alternative, it did give a choice, though within the Democratic party. In a measure, the primary system operated to prevent the bursting of the bonds of party, for the controversy between highlands and lowlands was so great that not even a hallowed tradition would have preserved party loyalty had it not been for the opportunity to let off steam inside the party. The primary system paved the way for Bleases, Heflins, Longs, Bilbos, and Talmadges. It created a device by which southern discontent and dissatisfaction might be discharged upon an imaginary foe. Again and again, the poor farmer, the dissatisfied hillman, had the vicarious satisfaction of reasserting his supremacy over the even poorer Negroes, but at no time did he achieve a real victory over the ancient and real foe of himself and his fellows, namely, poverty and exploitation.

This means we must examine the real nature of the South economically and socially and see what outlets for unrest there are in politics. Once more we turn to the fateful years following Lee's surrender. In a period of reconstruction following another war perhaps we can more clearly understand the turn of events in the period 1860-70. When people are tired and war-weary they are not specially creative; they do not seek and blaze new trails but rather look to the old ways. In other words, what happens is more likely to be an expedient than a plan, it is a drift rather than a design, an accident rather than an achievement. Such we may well call the land tenure system which succeeded the slave plantation. In 1865 people had to eat and food was scarce. In the months from April to June it was necessary to look to the next harvest. There was land and there was labor, but precious little capital. Land and labor were put up as credit to obtain capital. In effect, land and labor have been doing the same thing ever since as the seasons roll around to the time when cotton, corn, and tobacco need to be planted. The landlord had his land which he could pledge to get seed, food, and tools for the production of a crop. The worker had only his labor and this he must pledge to the landlord who, in turn, pledged his land to the credit merchant or the banker. The land would be there all during the season; it was fixed and constant.

But what of the worker? In no small measure, the "labor" legislation of the South since 1865 has been an effort to fix security for a worker's pledge. A migratory group without tradition of the sacredness of promises upon which capitalism is allegedly founded, southern workers both black and white have not a reputation for dependability, especially in harvest season when the going wage rate may likely rise. Accordingly, landowners have sought through legislation to substitute as nearly as possible a replica of the slave system. At first, the legislatures made it a criminal offense for a person under contract to break his contract of employment to accept another. This, it was expected, would add a sanction to the civil penalty for breach where the absence of worldly goods made the penalty largely illusory. However, this simple and direct approach ran afoul of the federal constitution and federal legislation against peonage.[17] Consequently, considerable ingenuity had to be exercised in legislative inventiveness. Eventually the legislatures came up with the answer in the form of so-called inducement or enticement to breach statutes.

These laws do not directly fix the penalty upon the worker but upon another employer who seeks to induce the worker to break his contract. Under these acts it is a misdemeanor for any employer to offer employment to any employee currently employed, usually under written contract. The injured employer may not only secure civil damages for the wrong done him but may have criminal penalties applied as well.[18] The Mississippi Supreme Court has described the nature of the statutes very well.

> . . . . [The law] was designed to stabilize the agricultural industry, the chief industry of the state, and to this end the Legislature penalized all efforts of one farmer to persuade the tenants of another farmer to "jump their contracts." The agricultural labor of the state is overwhelmingly of African descent. They are credulous and fickle, and easily persuaded, and thus for the common good this statute was enacted.[19]

These laws explain the occasional display of force by sheriffs' posses on the borders of a county during cotton picking time to prevent potential employers of other regions from offering employment at a season of competitive high wage rates. So far, the highest courts of the southern states have upheld the constitutionality of these statutes with a single exception. The Court of Appeals of Kentucky alone has declared statutes of this type to be abridgments of a free and competitive economy.[20] In other states the relative frequency with which cases have arisen and have been carried to the higher courts supports the conclusion that these laws have more than an occasional use as a weapon in the bargaining process. Whether such legislation would withstand a test in a federal court is unknown, for no case has ever gone to one.

The feudal flavor of these inducements to breach laws is shown by the fact that they are fundamentally based upon the Statute of Laborers first passed by the English Parliament in 1347 to prevent a rise in wages after the Black Death had depleted the labor supply. The whole conception of master-servant is a residue from the medieval guild system and its application in a twentieth century capitalist system is highly extraneous, to say the least.[21]

Other legal devices have occasionally been resorted to. In Arkansas a few years ago a sheriff who was also a planter and a political boss arrested a considerable number of Negroes for vagrancy during the height of the cotton picking season. An obliging justice of the peace found the offending persons guilty and turned them over to work for the planter sheriff for thirty days in order to save the county from having to board them in the jail for the period. Unfortunately, a New Dealish federal marshal intervened and arrested the sheriff for violating the federal peonage act. The sheriff-planter was considerably nonplussed when he was convicted in federal court and sentenced to solitary confinement by a federal judge who was a former governor of the commonwealth and, of course, a Democrat!

Enough of this type of legislation has been shown to exhibit the character of post-bellum efforts to reincorporate the feudal principle of unfree labor in the political economy of the South after the passage of the Thirteenth Amendment. In other words, the nature of the agricultural economy, the character of its labor force, the absence of capital and the presence of a manorial-feudal-plantation tradition glamorized in the mellow memories of a mystic and mythical golden age served to perpetuate a system of land tenure which resembled the slave economy in existence prior to the war. To keep this kind of economy meant that the agencies of the state must not be used by workers to enhance their bargaining power. A free franchise would have made possible the modification of the legislation just described. Under the circumstances, it was deemed necessary by the governing class to prevent the enfranchisement of the great bulk of workers, whether white or colored. The symbols of sovereignty as well as the control of the traditions and organization of the Democratic party must be kept in the hands of the governing elite.

In conclusion, I trust I have demonstrated that the term "party" used to describe a working agency of government no longer applies to what is called the Democratic party in the South. The Democratic party has become a symbol of a way of life, fundamentally undemocratic socially, politically, and economically. The Democratic party is an order into which one is born; it is a tradition which symbolizes a long-since outgrown past whose perpetuation is a part of a creed of loyalty to one's forebears, a species of ancestor worship without meaning in contemporary political action. As an order, the Democratic party has a creed inherited from the nonindustrial past, a set of heroes including Jefferson and Jackson and perhaps Woodrow Wilson and Franklin D. Roosevelt, but the ancient institution is not a going concern as a political party which presents alternative programs to that offered by a big business dominated Republican party. The old Democratic party is a failure unless it changes from its traditional role of preserving the *status quo* in the South established somewhat accidentally in the reconstruction era of 1865–95.

In similiar fashion the Republican party in the South is a regional opposition to the dominant Democratic party. In no small measure, southern republicanism preserves a pioneer small hill farmer resentment to lowland plantation agriculture. It preserves the memory of the Civil War, the loyalty to the Union and opposition to either big agriculture or urbanism. Both political parties in the South are anachronisms with their eyes fixed on the past, not on the future. Both are embalmed traditions rather than vital functioning organisms which give expression to the dynamic forces of modern industrial life

II

VOTING IN THE SOUTH: PAST, PRESENT, AND FUTURE

WHO should vote? To make this inquiry is to go to the heart of the problem of government. Should the few or the many determine the policies and select the officials of government? To inquire whether there should be a broad base to the franchise is to ask a question generally answered in the nineteenth century. It was a part of the general spread of the idea of the common man's worth generated in the late eighteenth century and surely well nigh universal by the beginning of the twentieth. Universal suffrage for males and then for all adults has come with the ending of World War II in Europe. Even the Latin countries have now accepted woman suffrage.

Universal suffrage is part of the democratic tradition which we are seeking to export to the Germans, the Japanese, and for that matter, to all the world. At the risk of possible physical conflict we are insisting that the remote and backward areas of Europe should adopt universal suffrage with a secret ballot. It is not too long since we attempted to teach several of the Caribbean countries the virtues of universal suffrage at the point of the bayonet. Although we may have changed our pedagogical technique slightly, we still lecture our Latin neighbors upon the sacredness of the secret ballot. Our recognition policy has in no small measure been based upon the principle of the consent of the governed as evidenced in the choice of a government by popular election.

Upon what hypothesis is the franchise based? The Constitution of Tennessee states, in Article I, Section 1, "That all power is inherent in the people, and all free governments are founded on their authority, and instituted for their peace, safety, and happiness. . . . ." Section 5 of the same article declares:

> That elections shall be free and equal, and the right of suffrage, as hereinafter declared, shall never be denied to any person entitled thereto, except upon a conviction by a jury of some infamous crime, previously ascertained and declared by law and judgment thereon by court of competent jurisdiction.

Who are the people? When are elections "free and equal"? What is the "right of suffrage"?

First of all, we must determine a theory of suffrage which will govern conferring the right to vote. A careful student has analyzed five separate theories of suffrage.[1] First is the ancient view developed in the Greek city-state that the vote belonged to citizens even as participation in its life belonged to members of a family. Since the state was only an extension of the family all citizens voted by virtue of their existence as citizens. They were organic parts of a tightly knit whole; hence, citizenship without voting was inconceivable. The city-state conception gave way to the feudal theory that voting was a tenurial right belonging to the ownership of landed property. This serves to corroborate the point made previously that man's relation to the land was the essence of feudalism. In the third place came the idea that the vote belonged to all men *qua* men, that voting was a natural right of man as much as liberty of speech or freedom of religion. Undoubtedly this is the most popular theory, even today, and certainly undergirding any wide grant of the franchise is a belief in the natural rights idea. One of the best presentations of this point of view is that of Charles Sumner, who, in a letter to John Bright in 1867, wrote:

> . . . . It cannot be that so important a question as whether a citizen shall have a voice in the government can depend on such narrow considerations and technicalities of property. Who but the learned can ever know how to define a "compound householder"? It seems to me that the present success of Dis-

raeli will drive you to place the suffrage on absolute principles, where I am sure it belongs. For a long time I was perplexed by the subtlety so often presented that the suffrage was a "privilege" and not a "right," and being a "privilege" it was subject to such limitations as the policy or good-will of the legislature chose to impose. The more I think of it, the more it seems to me an essential right, which government can only regulate and guard, but cannot abridge. All just government stands on "the consent of the governed." Starting with this principle from our Declaration of Independence, I see no other conclusion than that every citizen having a proper residence must be a voter. If it be said that, then, the ignorant man has the same electoral weight as the intelligent, I reply: "No; each has the same vote; but the other exercises an influence over the result,—in other words, over other votes,—in proportion to his intelligence." In the vote itself all are equal.[2]

Obviously this hypothesis is untenable, for the vote would come at birth and would *ipso facto* belong to all human beings regardless of color, race, sex, property, education, or reason. This is so clearly untrue as to require little comment. The Alabama Supreme Court has correctly held that:

. . . . political suffrage is not an absolute or natural right, but is a privilege conventionally conferred upon the citizen by the sovereignty. There can be practically no such thing as universal suffrage, and it is believed that no such theory is recognized among any people. . . . . No one can lawfully vote under any government of laws except those who are expressly authorized by law.[3]

A fourth, and a more scientific approach is that the vote is an *office* conferred upon those qualified to perform its duties. This idea carefully distinguishes the electorate, that is, those with the office of voting, from the mass of the population.

From necessity the question of substantive qualifications for the office of voting is raised. Clearly the inhibitions in the federal constitution against such nonrational factors as race, color, previous condition of servitude, and sex are well based, but these are negative restrictions upon the states rather than the affirmative qualifications. In passing, it may be said that the South has never willingly accepted the first three and only very reluctantly the last for few Southern states wished to relinquish a feudal status for women. Is the possession or ownership of property an evidence of qualification for exercising the office of voting? No one has ever been able to set up an objective standard to prove that ownership of property either indicates superior intelligence or inherent nobility of character. The argument of Tom Paine seems conclusive.

> .... Wealth is no proof of moral character; nor proverty of the want of it; on the contrary, wealth is often the presumptive evidence of dishonesty. .... When a broodmare shall fortunately produce a foal or a mule, that, by being worth the sum in question, shall convey to the owner the right of voting .... in whom does the origin of such a right exist? Is it in the man, or in the mule?[4]

In fact, Rousseau argued persuasively that any *private* as distinguished from a *public* or general *will* should be prohibited. The electorate must seek the general good or public welfare rather than private interest.[5] Certainly the payment of taxes, whether poll taxes or not, shows no affirmative qualification for the office of voting. Finally, a logical argument may be made for sufficient education to be able to determine what the public good is; for sufficient rationality to distinguish between bald emotional appeals to prejudice or hate, and arguments based upon fact and logic; and for enough character to enable the formation of a will to action. Unfortunately, we have no sound criteria to determine the possession of such intelligence, rationality, or character, even if we were able to define precisely these intangibles. What little evidence we have certainly indicates that what passes for "education" in the current folklore does not make for such intelligence, rationality, or character. Indeed, in England, the university constituencies of Oxford and Cambridge are remembered chiefly for their return of notoriously conservative political hacks.

Should even literacy be established as a prerequisite? *Prima facie* a good case can be made for such a requirement, but again there is little evidence that literacy is equivalent to the sound judgment which experience may produce in the unsophisticated as well as in the sophisticated. Two other arguments may be advanced against a literacy test. First, there is the problem of administration. Who will administer such tests? Election officials? Political sophistication and familiarity with the use of such tests in southern states immediately produces a loud "no" for answer. Should the schools be the administrative agency? Surely the schools of the South are already too closely connected with the personal and partisan political process to invite further intimacy. Finally, is the completion of a certain grade in school an adequate criterion? Certainly there is no guarantee that such an achievement will produce functional literacy, either in a narrow or broader sense, our schools being what they are. Suppose, however, we were to require economic literacy as a prerequisite for voting. Would advocacy of a protective tariff or a sales tax disfranchise one? The practical difficulties are such that no effective argument can be presented in favor of any workable set of literacy qualifications. Will any college faculty member who has endured the *ennui* of a long number of faculty meetings and the tedium and feebleness of logic there manifested contend that more intelligence, nobility of character, or rationality of decision are in evidence in a group of doctors of philosophy than in a trade union, a Ladies Aid Society, a Farm Bureau meeting, or, for that matter, in any assembly of illiterates on the western frontier? Sophistication is not noted for producing selflessness or keen awareness of the general good.

This leaves us with one more theory of the franchise, which has been called the ethical theory. It is briefly as follows: the exercise of the franchise, as membership on juries, is a valuable social and civic experience which may well develop a critical faculty in individuals and, hence, a more elevated society. The consciousness of the possession of a right to exercise a choice may well enhance self-respect, encourage study, produce a certain objectivity, all of which are surely desirable traits in citizens. These considerations, though inconclusive, should be of great weight in determining which people should vote. On this basis the noninclusion of poor whites and Negroes alike may be pointed out as a further contribution to their degradation. John Stuart Mill has best expressed this point of view.

> .... It by is political discussion that the manual labourer, whose employment is a routine, and whose way of life brings him in contact with no variety of impressions, circumstances, or ideas, is taught that remote causes, and events which take place far off, have a most sensible effect even on his personal interests; and it is from political discussion, and collective political action, that one whose daily occupations concentrate his interests in a small circle round himself, learns to feel for and with his fellow-citizens, and becomes consciously a member of a great community. But political discussions fly over the heads of those who have no votes, and are not endeavoring to acquire them. Their position, in comparison with the electors, is that of the audience in a court of justice, compared with the twelve men in the jury-box. It is not *their* suffrages that are asked, it is not their opinion that is sought to be influenced; the appeals are made, the arguments addressed, to other than them; nothing depends on the decision they may arrive at, and there is no necessity and very little inducement to them to come to any. Whoever, in an otherwise popular government, has no vote, and no prospect of obtaining it, will either be a permanent malcontent, or will feel as one whom the general affairs of society do not concern; for whom they are to be managed by others; who "has no business with the laws except to obey them," nor with public interests and concerns except as a looker-on. What he will know or care about them from this position may partly be measured by what an average woman of the middle class knows and cares about politics, compared with her husband or brothers.[6]

In view of these theoretical considerations, let us examine the origin and growth of the poll tax and other methods of disfranchisement in the South. Historically these restrictions belong not so much to the Reconstruction Era as to the Populist period and the developments growing out of the Bryan Crusade. The impact of the agricultural depression of the 1870's and 1880's was so great that the poor farmers, owners and tenants alike, in the West were being driven from their allegiance to the Republican party and in the South Tom Watson was shaking to its very foundation the loyalty of poor farmers, black and white, to the Democratic party.[7] It may be pointed out here that thousands of Negroes voted the Democratic ticket in some measure because of their loyalty to their former masters and, in part, because of a lack of sophistication with respect to issues. Wade Hampton had correctly predicted this result.

> No harm would be done the South by Negro suffrage. The old owners would cast the votes of their people almost as absolutely and securely as their own. If Northern men expected in this way to build up a northern party in the South, they were greatly mistaken. They would only be multiplying the power of the old and natural leaders of Southern politics by giving a vote to every former slave. Heretofore such men had served their masters only in the fields; now they would do no less faithful service at the polls. If the North could stand it, the South could. For himself, he should make no special objection to Negro suffrage as one of the terms of reorganization, and if it came, he did not think the South would have much cause to regret it.[8]

The white farmers of the Piedmont saw in the Negroes a group of voters manipulated by the Black Belt whites or Bourbons. The plantation owners, however, saw with consternation the possibility that the Negroes would join with the poor whites to make a permanent alliance and an effective majority hostile to what the Black Belt Bourbons regarded as their own interests. The possibility of a new farmer-labor party composed of both blacks and whites is shown by a large vote the Populists received in 1892. Weaver, the Populist nominee, took the following percentages of all votes cast in the Southern states:

Alabama	36.60
Arkansas	8.07
Florida	16.06
Georgia	19.17
Kentucky	6.92
Louisiana	5.30
Mississippi	19.42
Missouri	7.59
North Carolina	15.94
South Carolina	3.42
Tennessee	8.92[9]

This danger combined with the always inviting temptation of the Populists to join the Republicans to wrest control from the Democrats seriously threatened the post-bellum *status quo*. It is the irony of the American political party system that the agrarian reformers had to join with the big business dominated Republican party to get control of their own state governments, or, because of their fear of the Negroes, surrender to the reactionary group in control of the Democratic party. It was between 1890 and 1908 that the franchise-restricting legislation and constitutional changes were made. In Alabama, as John B. Clark in his *Populism in Alabama* says:

> An acrimonious fight ensued over the advisability of a constitutional convention whereby the hide bound document formed in 1875 might be so changed as to allow the state to develop in all respects. All agreed that changes were needed but many doubted the wisdom of stirring the question now. Speaker Pettus introduced a bill which after long, slow sledding was killed. *Especially did the Populists oppose any attempt to change the constitution because it would cost too much money and be only an effort to rob the Negro of his vote.*[10]

The leading student of Populism, Professor John D. Hicks, writes:

> The situation was different in the South, but it was no less unfavorable to the perseverance of Populism. There the unholy alliance with the Republicans drove many third-party adherents back to the Democratic fold; while others, especially the more radical leaders, who could never hope to recover their standing in Democratic circles, drifted over to the Republicans. Furthermore, the absurdity of fusing with the Democrats in one section of the country and with the Republicans in another could not fail to break down Populist morale. Obviously an enduring party could not be built upon such shifting sands.
>
> The breakdown of Populism in the South is associated closely with the results of the fusion experiment in North Carolina. There the Republicans and Populists had won in the election of 1896 not only the legislature and the state offices but many local and county offices as well. In some of the eastern counties, where the bulk of the Republican voters were negroes, this meant negro officeholders in large numbers. Whole counties were said to be "negroized," and the horrors of Reconstruction, if not exactly repeated, were at least feared. A white Republican postmaster at Wilmington, North Carolina, warned his party that it was permitting too many negroes to hold office. With thirty-six colored magistrates in the county, a colored register of deeds, and some colored appointees of the national administration, he felt certain that to avoid a conflict between the races the local offices must be promptly turned over to the whites. A Raleigh correspondent wrote to the *Atlanta Constitution* that the negroes, with no less than a thousand members of their race holding office in North Carolina, were preparing to make the state a place of refuge for their kind from all over the South; and this item, copied by most of the North Carolina papers as a startling revelation of the truth, aroused intense excitement throughout the state.
>
> Even the Populists were affected. If the existence of a third party was to mean in practice that the negroes were to have the upper hand, many reformers were ready to abandon their third-party tickets. Democrats announced boldly, as the elections of 1898 approached, that they were determined to overthrow negro rule, "peaceably if possible, but by revolution if they must." Populists were urged to return to a Democratic party that was now, so it was alleged, thoroughly renovated

and in entire harmony with Populist principles. As an organization, however, the Populist party in North Carolina continued its cooperation with the Republicans, and in the election of 1898 the Democrats still had to face a powerful and well-united opposition.

But once the issue of white supremacy was successfully raised, the triumph of the Democrats was easy. In vain did the Populist leaders maintain that the Democratic leopard had not changed its spots; that all its protestations of reform were insincere. In vain did the third-party orators defend fusion as the only practical means of obtaining results and saving the party. "If we go in the middle of the road," said one of them, "which might be the best course for us to pursue if we could pursue it and live as an organization, the canvass will be made against our candidates by the Democratic party 'that you have no chance for election. Our candidates will be elected or the Republicans will be. You are simply not in it.' "[11]

However, Mississippi claims the distinction of being the first state to "solve" the problem. The official historian of the state in a series of volumes published in 1925 declares at one point,

> Mississippi was the first State in the Union to solve the problem of white supremacy in the South by constitutional means. The constitution of 1890 disfranchised the ignorant and vicious of both races, and placed the control of the State in the hands of its virtuous, intelligent citizenry.
>
> The early aspirations that found their way into the concrete legislation of Mississippi were to a large extent the practical fruitage of the Christian ideal of its people which since the State's early formation was implanted deep in their character. As a pioneer stock, they felt a dependence upon divine providence that was deep and genuine. Their conduct and thought were marked by a beautiful simplicity that comes of sincerity of purpose. The people of Mississippi would do well to hold fast to the types which the Confederate veteran and the woman of the Confederacy represent.[12]

We can only wonder if the historian included Theodore G. Bilbo in his exhibits of the products of enfranchising only the "virtuous, intelligent citizenry."

However, the enfranchisement of virtue and intelligence

seems to have encountered some difficulties for the same authority says:

> The clause of the franchise article which caused the keenest discussion was that which proposed to place certain educational and financial restrictions upon the right of suffrage. As the discussion progressed, it was soon seen that there was a vigorous minority which opposed a qualified suffrage. What was proposed as a radical check on the exercise of a pauper vote among the ignorant and degraded of the blacks would react materially upon the white vote. An educational qualification would exclude from the suffrage about five thousand white voters in a total white voting population of about 130,000. There were many illiterate white voters in the State, who had accumulated property and were taxpayers. A property qualification to be effectual would disfranchise a larger number of white voters. It was therefore considered problematic whether the imposition of such tests would improve the situation for the whites.[13]

Eventually, however, a happy solution was arrived at:

> A franchise article was finally formulated containing all the features of the provision finally adopted by the constitutional convention, except the postponement of the educational and understanding clause until January 1, 1892, instead of January 1, 1896, and the substitution of a $2.00 instead of a $3.00 poll tax.[14]

It was part of the astuteness of the framers of these disfranchising clauses that the funds from the poll tax were to be used for educational purposes. Enthusiasm for education was not too great, however, for when a sheriff made an effort to seize household furniture for the poll tax, the Supreme Court of Mississippi interpreted the statute with commendable frankness. The poll tax was not primarily a revenue measure, the court declared, but rather a franchise regulation. The court said the chief purpose of the 1890 constitutional convention was to disfranchise the Negro and keep within the federal constitution. To do so,

> .... the convention swept the circle of expedients to obstruct the exercise of the franchise of the negro race. By reason of

its previous condition of servitude and dependence, this race had acquired or accentuated certain peculiarities of habit, of temperament, and of character, which clearly distinguished it as a race from that of the whites,—a patient, docile people, but careless, landless, and migratory within narrow limits, without forethought, and its criminal members given rather to furtive offenses than to the robust crimes of the whites. Restrained by the federal constitution from discriminating against the negro race, the convention discriminated against its characteristics and the offenses to which its weaker members were prone. A voter who should move out of his election precinct, though only to an adjoining farm, was declared ineligible until his new residence should have continued for a year. Payment of taxes for two years at or before a date fixed many months anterior to an election is another requirement, and one well calculated to disqualify the careless. Burglary, theft, arson, and obtaining money under false pretenses were declared to be disqualifications, while robbery and murder and other crimes in which violence was the principal ingredient were not.[15]

After reviewing the proceedings of the constitutional convention somewhat in detail, the court concluded,

.... It is evident, therefore, that the convention had before it for consideration two antagonistic propositions: One, to levy a poll tax as a revenue measure, and to make its payment compulsory; the other, to impose the tax as one of many devices for excluding from the franchise a large number of persons, which class it was impracticable wholly to exclude, and not desirable wholly to admit. In our opinion, the clause was primarily intended by the framers of the constitution as a clog upon the franchise, and secondarily and incidentally only as a means of revenue.[16]

Hence, if the language of the constitution was susceptible of two constructions,

.... it must be so construed as to carry into effect the purpose of the convention. It is evident that, the more payment of the tax is made compulsory, the greater will be the number by whom it will be paid, and therefore, the less effectual will be the clause for the purpose it was intended.[17]

In other states the poorer whites did not surrender without protest. There was vigorous disagreement among the delegates to the Tennessee convention in 1870 to the provision requiring a poll tax payment as a condition precedent to voting. Let one petition among several speak eloquently its own indictment of the poll tax system.

> The undersigned cannot satisfy their sense of duty to themselves and to their constituents without stating in full the reasons that prompted their vote against the 1st Section of the 4th Article of the Amended Constitution, known as the Franchise Section. That section requires that every voter *before he can vote* shall produce "satisfactory evidence" to the judges of election *that he has paid his poll-tax.* Had it not been for this required prepayment of the poll-tax the undersigned would gladly have voted for said section. Their constituents now vote without any tax restriction, and they cannot consent to impose such restriction upon them; they favor the removal of *all* restrictions, and not the creation of new ones.
>
> But the undersigned are firm believers in the doctrine that suffrage is a *right* and not a *privilege*—as much a right as life, liberty or property—a right not to be limited and not to be restricted except as to age, time and place; and above all, a right not to be bestowed on the rich *in preference* to the poor. Suffrage is the political means of self-defense, and the disfranchised man is, or soon will be, a slave. Such being their cardinal doctrine, the undersigned would enumerate the following minor reasons for their vote:
>
> 1st. *The right to restrict the elective franchise implies the right to destroy it.*
>
> If *one* obstacle can be placed between the voter and the ballot-box, the entire road can be closed. If one qualification can be required, so can *another*, so can *many*. Is the payment of money a better pre-requisite for *voting* than is proof of loyalty, or of intelligence or morality?
>
> 2d. *The required pre-payment of the poll-tax is an unjust discrimination against the poor man.* What is taxation? Taxation is the price of protection. But the poor man, having but little property, needs but little protection. And yet, by said section, the poor man has *just the same tax* to pay before he can vote as the rich man.
>
> 3d. *The required pre-payment of the poll-tax as a qualification for voting is more oppressive to the rich than a property qualification.*

Where there is a property qualification the voter can vote and pay his poll-tax afterwards. But here he must pay his poll-tax before he can vote at all. In truth, this whole thing is nothing but a property qualification in disguise.

4th. *The required pre-payment of the poll-tax will give the rich candidate an unjust but great advantage over a poor candidate.*

The rich candidate, in person or through friends, can pay the poll-tax of every poor man favorable to his election, while the poor men, favorable to the poor candidate, will in many cases be unable to vote. And here the door is opened to infinite bribery and infinite corruption in Tennessee politics.

5th. *The required pre-payment of the poll-tax will enable a partisan tax collector to disfranchise many voters.* Suppose the tax-collector should refuse to receive the poll-tax from certain voters, or should absent himself, for political purposes, or should resign or die shortly before an election, how easily could he thus change the result of an election, and defeat the true will of the people. We see here commissioners of registration with a *new* name!

6th. *The required pre-payment of the poll-tax only substitutes a tax receipt for the present voting certificate.* The voter has to produce "satisfactory evidence" to the judges of election that he has paid his poll-tax. What is "satisfactory evidence"? It is legal evidence sufficient to satisfy the *judicial* mind; and that legal evidence the courts will quickly declare must be a tax receipt, the most odious of voting certificates.

7th. *The required pre-payment of the poll-tax will enable partisan judges of election to disfranchise legal voters.* Democratic judges will be "satisfied" with little or no "evidence" when a Democrat offers his vote; but will require the most "satisfactory evidence," to-wit: a tax receipt, when a Republican offers his vote, and *vice versa*. How monstrous the inducement to corruption!

8th. *The required pre-payment of the poll-tax will be the mother of infinite contests and strife in elections.*

In consequence of the possible frauds above mentioned being actually perpetrated, many lawful voters will be practically disfranchised, and many unlawful voters allowed to vote. Fraudulent tax receipts will be forged. Perjury will usher in many a vote. Bribery will luxuriate around the ballot-box. Poor men will stand back with a sigh, while the rich put in their votes. Challenges will be endless; and the resulting strife and bad feeling infinite. Nobody will be satisfied. The ballot will lose its dignity. Elections will become a farce; and—but we prefer to drop the curtain upon the last scene in this horrid drama.[18]

This dark prophecy has by no means been inaccurate, though the effectiveness of franchise restrictive legislation is difficult to measure. The fact that voting declined after the enactment of poll tax and educational requirements is clear. About a decade ago, the author made a study of farm tenancy in what is generally called the Big Bend of the Tennessee River. Included were twenty counties, ten in Alabama, seven in Tennessee, and three in Mississippi. His conclusion was that:

> The effectiveness of this legislation and of administrative practices under it is shown by the significant decline in voting after the passage of poll tax and registration laws in Alabama. It is further evidenced by the close connection between the small percentage of the voting population which votes and the high percentage of tenancy. By and large where there was a large number of owner operators there was a relatively high percentage voting, and where there was a large number of tenants there was a small percentage voting, even after discounting the negro voters.
>
> The relation between tenancy and the percentage of white males voting in 1904 is expressed by the negative correlation of −.36. Though unreliable for as few as twenty counties, this negative coefficient shows a tendency for a high proportion of tenancy to accompany a low percentage of votes in the counties of the Big Bend. Neither would the presence of a large number of negroes in a number of counties account for this fact.
>
> Finally, the relation shown to exist in 1904 between high tenancy and low vote is confirmed in 1932. Where in 1904 a correlation of −.36 existed between tenancy and vote, the coefficient for 1932 is −.70, a reliable indication that the two vary inversely.[19]

Further evidence of the disfranchising effect of the new provisions is shown by comparison of voting behavior in Kentucky and Tennessee.

TABLE 1

Percentage of Adult Population Voting in Presidential Election Years, Kentucky and Tennessee, 1872-1940

Year	Kentucky Percentage of Adult Population Voting (Male before 1920)	Tennessee Percentage of Adult Population Voting (Male before 1920)
1872	55	55
1876	68	64
1880	65	61
1884	64	64
1888	76	71
Poll tax begins in Tennessee		
1892	72	58
1896	88	67
1900	87	54
1904	79	46
1908	87	48
1912	76	45
1916	88	48
1920	63	31
1924	54	20
1928	61	23
1932	62	24
1936	56	28
1940	57	30

Source: *Hearings before Subcommittee of the Committee of The Judiciary, United States Senate, 77th Congress, 2nd Session, on S. 1280* (Washington: U. S. Government Printing Office, 1942), pp. 55-60.

I think we may finish this general review with the conclusion of a careful survey made in 1928 in Virginia.

> We may conclude by saying that the suffrage provisions of the Constitution of 1902 have resulted in eliminating the negro: that the elimination of the negro has brought a feeling of security and an attitude of indifference among the whites; that the predicted independence of thought and action among the white voters, relieved of the negro menace, has failed to materialize; and that, as a result, the State lacks a real party of opposition, is still solidly Democratic, and has delivered itself into the hands of less than 10 per cent of its citizens.[20]

In the effort to narrow the franchise southern Democrats have constantly been confronted with constitutional limits set by our federal constitution. The process of enlarging the rights of federal citizens has been one of confining the freedom of operations of political parties. In the first place, the United States Supreme Court struck down a Texas statute which forbade Negroes to participate in a Democratic primary.[21] To do so the court had to overrule by inference its decision in the *Newberry* case[22] that a primary was not an election. Texas eagerly came forward with another attempt, this time an authorization given by the legislature to the political parties to regulate their own internal organization. This act likewise ran afoul of the Fourteenth Amendment and was held invalid.[23] Accordingly the Texas legislature, acting on a judicial hint from Mr. Justice Cardozo, repealed all statutory mention of exclusion by the parties but left the machinery for a primary system. This legislation was judicially approved in 1935.[24]

Subsequently, however, the United States Supreme Court has been "reconstructed" and the majority has expressly overruled its 1935 decisions, holding that since the state set up the procedure for primaries, it was evident that Texas was providing the device (i.e., the parties were agents of the state) by which evasion of the inhibitions of the Fourteenth and Fifteenth Amendments might be brought about.[25] Finally, South Carolina in order to escape the seemingly inevitable, repealed all constitutional and statutory mention of primaries leaving internal party regulation completely free of state control. The Georgia legislature took similar action but a gubernatorial veto intervened. Within recent months a federal district court has looked behind the legal façade in South Carolina and declared its latest action ineffective to accomplish its purpose because violative of federal statutes.[26]

In other words, the federal courts are showing a startling tendency to disregard the age old tradition that justice is blind. It would appear that the technique of clever evasion of federal constitutional inhibitions has about reached the limits of legal inventiveness. The situation will have to be confronted affirmatively and not negatively. Some suggestions of a positive nature will be offered in a later chapter.

The constitutionality of the poll tax was presented to the United States Supreme Court clearly for the first time in 1937. The court unanimously sustained its validity as a prerequisite to voting,[27] but the *Breedlove* case did not distinguish between the use of the tax as a prerequisite in a state and in a federal election. Since that time a new court has taken over with a tendency to expand very greatly the rights of a federal citizen. It is not at all certain that the tax might not be held a burden on the exercise of a federal right in view of the arguments developed in the *Classic* case.[28]

Finally, we come to the thorny subject of the respective powers of the federal and state governments over the franchise. It has been the general practice for lawyers and political scientists to state categorically that the authority to determine the qualifications of voters is exclusively in the hands of the states. Article I, Section 2 of the federal constitution reads:

> The House of Representatives shall be composed of members chosen every second year by the *people* of the several states and the *electors* in each state shall have the qualifications requisite for electors of the most numerous branch of the State legislature.[29]

Section 4 of the same article provides that:

> The times, places, and manner of holding elections for Senators and Representatives shall be prescribed in each state by the Legislature thereof; but the Congress may at any time by law make or alter such regulations, except as to the places of choosing Senators.

It is now contended by the proponents of a federal act outlawing the prescription of a poll tax as a prerequisite to voting that under this authority Congress may act. The basis of the argument rests primarily upon the decision of the

United States Supreme Court in the now famous *Classic* case. The issue involved was whether persons who had failed properly to count votes in a Democratic primary in Louisiana might be convicted for depriving a person of a right secured by the federal law under the federal constitution. The court held that a conviction would be sustained. The language of the majority opinion written by Mr. Justice Stone is clear:

> .... The right of the people to choose, whatever its appropriate constitutional limitations, where in other respects it is defined, and the mode of its exercise is prescribed by state action in conformity to the Constitution, is a right established and guaranteed by the Constitution and hence is one secured by it to those citizens and inhabitants of the state entitled to exercise the right.[30]

The majority opinion goes on to say:

> Obviously included within the right to choose, secured by the Constitution, is the right of qualified voters within a state to cast their ballots and have them counted at Congressional elections.[31]

Further on the court declares:

> Unless the constitutional protection of the integrity of "elections" extends to primary elections, Congress is left powerless to effect the constitutional purpose, and the popular choice of representatives is stripped of its constitutional protection save only as Congress, by taking over the control of state elections, may exclude from them the influence of the state primaries.[32]

The three dissenting judges were in agreement on the point of constitutional power, though disagreeing on a point of application of a criminal statute. The language of Mr. Justice Douglas who spoke for the dissenting justices is even more comprehensive in its scope than that of the majority. After quoting from the federal constitution, Article I, Sections 2 and 4, and the so-called "necessary and proper" clause, he goes on to say:

> .... Those sections are an arsenal of power ample to protect Congressional elections from any and all forms of pollution.

The fact that a particular form of pollution has only an indirect effect on the final elections is immaterial. The fact that it occurs in a primary election or nominating convention is likewise irrelevant. The important consideration is that the Constitution should be interpreted broadly so as to give to the representatives of a free people abundant power to deal with all the exigencies of the electoral process. It means that the Constitution should be read so as to give Congress an expansive implied power to place beyond the pale acts which, in their direct or indirect effect, impair the integrity of Congressional elections. For when corruption enters, the election is no longer free, the choice of the people is affected. To hold that Congress is powerless to control these primaries would indeed be a narrow construction of the Constitution, inconsistent with the view that that instrument of government was designed not only for contemporary needs but for the vicissitudes of time.[33]

At another point he speaks even more sweepingly:

Free and honest elections are the very foundation of our republican form of government. Hence any attempt to defile the sanctity of the ballot cannot be viewed with equanimity. As stated by Mr. Justice Miller in *Ex parte Yarbrough*, 110 U.S. 651, 666, "the temptations to control these elections by violence and corruption" have been a constant source of danger in the history of all republics. The acts here charged, if proven, are of a kind which carries that threat and are highly offensive. Since they corrupt the process of Congressional elections, they transcend mere local concern and extend a contaminating influence into the national domain.[34]

It is on the basis of these arguments that the late Senator George W. Norris of Nebraska who originally thought such legislation to be unconstitutional, wrote a report for the Judiciary Committee of the Senate recommending the passage of a federal anti–poll tax law. The language is careful and well considered. It reads as follows:

The qualification of a voter is generally believed to have something to do with the capacity of a voter. We think it will be admitted by all that no State, or State legislature, would have the constitutional authority to disqualify a voter otherwise qualified to vote, by setting up a pretended "qualification" that in fact has nothing whatever to do with the real qualification of the voter. No one can claim that the provision of the Federal Constitution above quoted would give a legislature the right to say that no one should be entitled to vote unless, for instance, he had red hair, or had attained the age of 100 years, or any artificial pretended qualification which, in fact, had nothing to do with the capacity or real qualification of the voter.

The evil that the legislation seeks to correct is in effect that in taking advantage of the constitutional provision regarding qualifications, the States have no right to set up a perfectly arbitrary and meaningless pretended qualification which in fact, is no qualification whatever and is only a pretended qualification by which large numbers of citizens are prohibited from voting simply because they are poor. Can it be said, in view of the civilization of the present day, that a man's poverty has anything to do with his qualification to vote? Can it be claimed that a man is incapacitated from voting simply because he is not able to pay the fee which is required of him when he goes to vote? In other words, when States have prevented citizens from voting simply because they are not able to pay the amount of money which is stipulated shall be paid, can such a course be said to have anything to do with the real qualifications of the voter? Is it not a plain attempt to take advantage of this provision of the Constitution and prevent citizens from voting by setting up a pretended qualification which, in fact, is no qualification at all?

We believe there is no doubt but that the prerequisite of the payment of a poll tax in order to entitle a citizen to vote has nothing whatever to do with the qualifications of the voter, and that this method of disfranchising citizens is merely an artificial attempt to use the language of the Constitution, giving the State power to set up qualifications, by using other artificial means and methods which in fact have no relation whatever to qualification.[35]

This argument is rather persuasive. The House of Representatives has accepted it repeatedly.[36] The Senate will do so if given the opportunity. Only the *liberum veto* of a filibuster has prevented action before now. How much longer will this minority weapon hold out?

We may conclude, then, that though the conception of

universal suffrage of all adults was taking hold and expanding during the last century throughout the world, for the last half century it has been contracting in the South. On the basis of the popular theory of the vote as a natural right or upon the view of the philosophers that the franchise is an ethical need for a highly developed citizenship, the South is running in the opposite direction. Though southern constitutions still contain noble professions about all power being inherent in the people, in practice sovereignty is the possession of a small group, from one-tenth to one-fifth of the potential electorate. This fact has been a source of no small amount of embarrassment to Secretary of State James Byrnes of South Carolina and Secretary of State George Marshall of Virginia. Our practice of disfranchisement of minorities, not to say majorities, in the South makes our diplomatic cheeks slightly red, or shall I say rosy, when we face the outside world to lecture them upon the virtues of political democracy.

III

THE GOVERNING CLASS OF A SOUTHERN COUNTY SEAT

*I*N OUR first discussion, we undertook to describe and analyze in broad terms the nature and character of the ante-bellum governing class of the South. It will be my purpose here to define more precisely the role and function of a governing class in general and in particular to examine the type of ruling elite which succeeded the old Bourbons in the South. We will want to get at the spiritual motif of this new class. First of all, let us look at the nature of a governing class in general. In all societies there is specialization of function and a hierarchy of values. An elite has been well defined by Harold D. Lasswell in his volume: *Politics; Who Gets What, When, How,* in the following fashion:

> The study of politics is the study of influence and the influential. The science of politics states conditions; the philosophy of politics justifies preferences. . . . .
> The influential are those who get the most of what there is to get. Available values may be classified as *deference, income, safety.* Those who get the most are *elite*; the rest are *mass.*[1]

The foremost student of the phenomena of the ruling class is Mosca, the late Italian senator and political scientist. He defines the problem in the following terms:

> Among the constant facts and tendencies that are to be found in all political organisms, one is so obvious that it is apparent to the most casual eye. In all societies—from societies that are very meagerly developed and have barely attained the dawnings of civilization, down to the most advanced and powerful societies—two classes of people appear—a class that rules and a class that is ruled. The first class, always the less numerous, performs all political functions, monopolizes power and

enjoys the advantages that power brings, whereas the second, the more numerous class, is directed and controlled by the first, in a manner that is now more or less legal, now more or less arbitrary and violent, and supplies the first, in appearance at least, with material means of subsistence and with the instrumentalities that are essential to the vitality of the political organism.[2]

In other words, in every society there is a hierarchy or a social pyramid. At the base of the pyramid are the masses, or, in Marxian terms, the proletariat, while at the top there is a small group, the elite or ruling class. Persons in academic life, in a bureaucracy, or in the army are familiar with this hierarchy beginning with the university president, bureau chief, general, *et al.* and running down through deans, division chiefs, section heads, to the lowly people who do the academic, bureaucratic or military K.P., such as clerks, mess sergeants, and professors. We have already seen that in the ante-bellum period this governing class in the South was the plantation owners with their ostentatiously simple mansions anchored and grounded in the soil, in an essentially feudal climate where the favorite literary figure was Sir Walter Scott.[3] The peculiar prestige of this governing class is shown in the fashion in which John Adams followed and bowed his knee to the leadership of George Washington, a fact noted with great interest by John's great-grandson, Henry Adams. Was it not one of the admirers of Daniel Webster who, watching Webster's devotion to Clay, remarked that if "Henry Clay were to start across hell on a rotten rail, Daniel Webster would be seen following him?"

The southern governing class was challenged in the period, 1860 to 1865, and the brightest flowers of its leadership were snuffed out in the vain effort to overcome the brutal facts of too much steel, too many men, and too much power. Who knows how many potential Calhouns, how many Jeffersons, and how many Madisons were buried at Shiloh, Gettysburg, Chancellorsville, and on other costly battlefields? One may ponder over how different a political future the South might have had if its most talented leadership potential had not been lost. Perhaps it was a similar loss in Germany which made Hitler a reality even as the South's loss made possible the Ku Klux Klan.

Nationally, the United States has never developed another political elite quite equal to that of its earlier founders, of which the landed gentry had furnished the larger number as well as the prototype. For one reason, the ethic of money getting, the motive of acquisitiveness, overcame the whole country. Nowhere do we have a better picture of the changes in the United States wrought by the Civil War than in Henry Adams' *Education*. Describing his return from England in 1868, he wrote:

> How much its character had changed or was changing, they could not wholly know, and they could but partly feel. For that matter, the land itself knew no more than they. Society in America was always trying, almost as blindly as an earthworm, to realize and understand itself; to catch up with its own head, and to twist about in search of its tail. Society offered the profile of a long, straggling caravan, stretching loosely towards the prairies, its few score of leaders far in advance and its millions of immigrants, Negroes, and Indians far in the rear, somewhere in archaic time. It enjoyed the vast advantage over Europe that all seemed, for the moment, to move in one direction, while Europe wasted most of its energy in trying several contradictory movements at once; but whenever Europe or Asia should be polarized or oriented towards the same point, America might easily lose her lead. Meanwhile each newcomer needed to slip into a place as near the head of the caravan as possible, and needed most to know where the leaders could be found.
>
> One could divine pretty nearly where the force lay, since the last ten years had given to the great mechanical energies—coal, iron, steam—a distinct superiority in power over the old industrial elements—agriculture, handwork and learning; but the result of this revolution on a survivor from the fifties resembled the action of the earthworm; he twisted about, in vain, to recover his starting-point; he could no longer see his own trail; he had become an estray; a flotsam or jetsam of wreckage; a

belated reveller, or a scholar-gipsy like Matthew Arnold's. His world was dead. Not a Polish Jew fresh from Warsaw or Cracow—not a furtive Yacoob or Ysaac still reeking of the Ghetto, snarling a weird Yiddish to the officers of the customs—but had a keener instinct, an intenser energy, and a freer hand than he—American of Americans, with Heaven knew how many Puritans and Patriots behind him, and an education that had cost a civil war. He made no complaint and found no fault with his time; he was no worse off than the Indians or the buffalo who had been ejected from their heritage by his own people; but he vehemently insisted that he was not himself at fault. The defeat was not due to him, nor yet to any superiority of his rivals. He had been unfairly forced out of the track, and must get back into it as best he could.[4]

Adams' description of the dilemma of the old New Englander was equally accurate for the old Southerner in the baffling New South. The old world was dead. There was no guide or signpost ahead. The Southerner knew no more where he was headed than the returned veteran of 1945 knows in this, the beginning of the third year of the atomic age. A governing class well adapted to govern in an agrarian or feudal period was peculiarly unfitted to function in a new, corporate, big business age, an era of industry and machines. The old class, largely destroyed, retreated into dignified retirement, sometimes to teach, sometimes to be college presidents, occasionally to write memoirs, now and then to do creative writing, perhaps in poetry or novel trying to recapture the "good old days" of a dead and gone past. Frequently, the old tradition would be brought out for a few friends to observe even as an elderly widow tenderly displays her crinkled and yellowed wedding gown.

The political center of gravity of the South changed from the countryside to the county seat between 1870 and 1900. The old manorial existence of self-sufficiency was gone. A desperate urge for cash which in the few first inflationary years of the postwar prosperity could be obtained in cotton became dominant. In a very short time, the pattern of the future was stamped upon the South. The county seat, the little urban center, took possession of the countryside and a gradual reorientation of values began. In its position as a colonial supplier of raw materials to the hungry maw of the industrial machinery of the new nation, the South had to find its level, and a very low level, indeed, it was.

The new governing class of the nation was a far cry from the old one. Where the old one emphasized politics, the new one concentrated on economics, trade, and industry, but especially on money. The old one manipulated men in government; the new one manipulated markets. The old one was generally quiet and dignified; it valued honor, polish, prestige, and tradition highly. The new class was raucous, vulgar, astute, deft in organization, and ruthless in method. The new "robber barons," the Vanderbilts, Rockefellers, Goulds, Morgans, Hills, Dukes, and Fords, had little respect for the old values.[5] They cherished power but sought it through production, exploitation, and speculation, rather than through oratory, argument, or politics. The visible government became a masquerade with a group of governors and senators and even presidents wearing the masks while behind the façade the new ruling class pulled the wires.

The lifeblood of this new society was credit and the merchants of credit, or bankers, who together with the great masters of technology and organization were the heart which controlled the supply of goods and services which flowed through the body politic and economic. The South had to adjust itself and it did. Somers, the English traveler, describing in 1870 the break up of old plantations in the Tennessee Valley of North Alabama, wrote:

> . . . . By-and-by there will be three or four flourishing farms where there was only one before. Pushing lawyers in the towns, and thrifty storekeepers, are also eking together good manageable farms, and cultivating them with fresh spirit and intelligence.[6]

He went on to point out that:

> Matrimony and planting are linked together by indissoluble

laws of nature, and herein probably arises one of the present difficulties of cotton growing in the Southern States.[7]

Women were beginning to be attracted to town and city living. He remarked that one sex pulled the other after it. In other words, the self-sufficient plantation broke down as the technology of sanitation, the improvement of bathrooms, and the building of schools began to give the town or county seat an advantage over the country as a way of life.

The results of this revolution in the social order in Alabama are well stated by John B. Clark:

> It has been said that the South in 1860 was the richest part of the country; in 1870, the poorest; in 1880, it showed signs of improvement; and by 1890 was regaining the position of 1860. Statistics show the tremendous change in the relative position of the farming class of 1860 and of the 'eighties and 'nineties. It was an almost complete reversal of positions from the top rung of the social and economic ladder to the nethermost rung. Before the war, the agricultural class had been prominent and prosperous, and in fact furnished from its ranks most of the lawyers, teachers, doctors, newspapermen, and clergymen. The farmer was a leader in local and state politics and his patronage might make or mar the fortune of the merchant who occupied an inferior role in society. But what changes came to pass within the three decades following Appomattox! The large plantation had been split into many smaller farms; the war had practically ruined him who owned land, for with his labor gone, with unprecedented public and private debts and tax burdens, with cotton still the chief crop, but worth less than it cost to produce it; with lawyers making big fees serving railroad companies, merchants, and corporations whose profits depended upon the agricultural class,—the farmer had lost his former prestige. This in itself was galling to his pride.[8]

That is to say, there was the formation of a new governing class, a county seat governing class. This group has come to determine the character and life of southern society. It is the values and ethics of this elite that I wish to examine in more detail. First of all, the fundamental ethic is pecuniary. The invariable popular epitaph of the county seat lawyer, merchant, banker, or editor is: how much was he worth?

Success or failure are apt to be measured in these terms. In part this is a successor of the feudal ethic of how many acres did he own. But something of the difference of emphasis is revealed in that the latter is measured in exchange value. Not infrequently the county seat elite measures success both in acres and in dollars. The farmer turned banker loses the feel of farm living. It is no longer a way of life. It has become a means of money making whose value is determined largely in the money income from the crop, or contemporaneously, it is a way of losing money and deducting from one's income tax. Farming has become a "business"—even the Colleges of Agriculture refer to it as such. The business approach has succeeded to the conception of feudal status.

The county seat farmer with a surplus of money or a strong source of credit may leap with great agility from crest to crest of economic cycles without dropping into the trough as real farmers have all too frequently done. In the words of Plunkitt of Tammany Hall, "he seen his opportunities and took 'em." However, he will be a sufficient farmer to join the Farm Bureau Federation and attend the annual state convention, perhaps be the local president. He may even be on the resolutions committee which urges the local legislature or national Congress to pass legislation curbing the closed shop and to put the labor leaders in their places.

The creed of this banker-merchant-farmer-lawyer-doctor-governing class is worthy of study. It explains more about southern politics than any analysis of structure can possibly do, though it is the decentralization of power into these semirural units which makes its existence possible. We must remember that there are nearly fifteen hundred county seats in the southern and border states—almost an average of one hundred to the state. The member of the governing group will be a joiner. He will probably belong to the church, in many cases be a leading member, probably an officer. He will observe the religious forms and pass the collection plate on Sunday. During the rest of the week his religion may be stored away unless he sings in the choir or belongs to the quartette which sings at funerals. Occasionally he may attend a church convention, and, upon demand, he can pray acceptably in public, frequently making up in quantity what his supplications lack in quality. He may even pray about the brotherhood of man, but in his day-to-day activities he may like others, overlook his conscience in the interest of business. "This is a business proposition, you know" will be his approach to a client and his reproach to a meddlesome conscience.

The county seat elite prides itself upon being practical. Upon examination this means accepting current political and social behavior without questioning its major premises. Getting ahead in business and the professions, making money, is its fundamental ethos. Though a member may distrust big business, at heart he admires it. His interests he conceives to be identical with those of all businessmen, hence he is intensely antilabor. He suspects labor leaders are communists, all in league with Moscow. His picture of labor was fixed in childhood. The hired man who picked cotton, hoed corn, cut tobacco, or milked the cows is his fixed stereotype of the working man. Workers are ignorant, illiterate, and drink too much. More than likely they are poor white trash. Their low estate is a punishment for moral dereliction and is a part of the natural order of things.

Shiftlessness is the child of idleness. Hard work is the salvation of the working class and this applies particularly to tenant farmers, who spend entirely too much time riding about in jalopies. If they would stay at home and work more closely, according to the oft repeated statements of retired farmers, they wouldn't be in debt all the time and would not be coming to landowners and merchants for credit and "furnish" so frequently. The small town merchant has little confidence in human nature. That all men are motivated by selfish ends, he accepts without question. Reforming or changing human nature he puts in the same class with reforming politics. To him, politics is a game of personal ambitions and conflicting economic self-interests. He regards all politics and politicians as corrupt. On occasion he may indulge in the game itself, for he understands perfectly well the role of influence in government and business. Though he preaches the doctrine of hard work, he practices "pull" whenever he can make it work. He is generally opposed to social change though technological change is readily approved. Progress to him means better automobiles, up-to-date refrigerators, the latest radio or other mechanical gadgets.

The county seat leader is not an intellectual and he distrusts the type. Schools are all right in their way and in their place, but the idea that the school should bring a new social order would shock him, if he should ever hear of it. School teaching is largely women's work except for coaching athletics. He may pay occasional lip service to the idea of better schools and he will cheerfully contribute to funds to buy uniforms, gifts, or awards for local athletes, who represent the "best little town on earth," for the chief stimulant to his local patriotism is the thrill he gets out of defeating the team from the nearest county seat. In this respect alone is he a sentimentalist, for he escapes from his daily routine and frustrating existence to be a boy again and vicariously relives his youth. He believes in education as he believes in God, the United States, and democracy. It is part of his folklore. That his mind needs to be challenged, his prejudices examined, and his stereotypes upset would make him uncomfortable, not to say angry. His legends are as necessary to his comfort as going in shirt sleeves on a hot day or his preference for his old bedroom slippers. Movies, radio, athletics, and his reading are all escapes, a kind of unconscious penance he pays for his drab and complacent existence. That there is anything better never occurs to him. He believes in the virtue of frequently exercising the body but never admits the same standard for his mind. He, of course, prides himself upon being a thinker, but rearranging his prejudices or stereotypes while fishing is his conception of higher thinking, though occassionally from the grist of his introversion may emerge an aphorism of singular wisdom, a gem distilled from his bitter experiences with people.

The small townsman belongs to an elite but is not an aristocrat. He offers lip service to the democratic credo of liberty, equality, and majority rule, but to his way of thinking liberty has nothing to do with labor leaders or college professors, and equality does not include people with black skins. Within his own caste he is relatively cautious in his associations but social life is largely left to his womenfolk who make up in snobbishness whatever the male members may lack. His "ladies" maintain their social ascendancy by industriously preoccupying themselves with their ancestors of the American Revolution or of the War between the States. Though thoroughly devoted to the romantic theory of marriage they usually control their emotions sufficiently to confine them to the proper social and economic stratum. Any departure from this accepted code is the cause of no little feminine discussion and occasionally social ostracism.

More than likely the long shadows of the pre-Civil War landed gentry will be cast more clearly in "society" than elsewhere. Some grand dame will sit on top of the local female hierarchy by virtue of holding title to many acres of land and the fact that her grandfather was a large and influential slaveholder. She is sort of a grand duchess in the community and the lesser ladies and knights fall in order in serried ranks within her social orbit. She rarely if ever demeans herself by participating in politics, but her unquestioned social ascendancy will lead the lesser lights to accept her loyalty to the Democratic party as her standard. As an Episcopalian or more seldom a Presbyterian, her standards of elegance dominate the church so that the wearers of blue denim and calico turn to more evangelical outlets for their religious instincts. Now and then they may cry out their frustrations in holiness meetings or indulge the white equivalent of Negro voodoo in snake handling and walking on fire.

The county seat governing class is caught between the industrial and agrarian mores. As farmers they are anchored in the soil by tradition and environment and they dislike instinctively big cities and big factories. The ancient grudge persists against the industrial way of life, but on the other hand their own business activities fit them into the ethic of cost accounting. They regard themselves as members of the governing class of the nation and particularly resent any efforts of trade union leaders to unseat them. They disliked Andrew Mellon and J. Pierpont Morgan, but they hate John L. Lewis and the C.I.O. Many of them hold memberships both in the Chamber of Commerce and the Farm Bureau Federation. The fact that older women with vested interests in land and public service securities represent normally somewhat more than half the population of the county seat accentuates the fears of any assault upon the property system. To these women, made more insecure frequently by widowhood, whose whole scheme of values is threatened by labor revolt or Negro emancipation, civil rights legislation is a fearsome thing. Reared in the code which placed a "lady" above household drudgery they feel their unquestioned right to cheap and servile black female labor. Civil rights is a personal issue to a southern lady, for it means that her own Liza or Mandy may ask wages above her somewhat slender means of payment or the coming of industry may mean her cook will go to a textile mill or possibly with better education actually become a stenographer or perhaps even a dietitian. Her whole social standing may be involved. Cheap black servants may even help Mississippi in recruiting college faculties, and ardent Yankee liberal advocates of civil rights and F.E.P.C. may find their ardor for reform cooled when they share in the benefits of the sheltered elite of the county seat. This is one of the subtle seductions of the southern way of life which

THE GOVERNING CLASS 49

not infrequently softens the most vigorous liberal enthusiasm and erodes the harshness of the most severe New England conscience.

The ghost of ante-bellum landed gentry hovers about Cottonton, Millville, and Tobaccoburg. The highest ambition of the most elite of the elite is to buy an estate and retire to the white columned mansions once owned by the slaveholders. Repainted and redecorated under eager and ambitious feminine supervision, the successful, both professional and mercantile, are reversing the trend of the seventies and eighties, for rural electrification has had one result, unanticipated by the New Deal, of reviving elegant country living as well as lifting the burdens of the humbler farmers. Here in a new technology the country club elite dreams of magnolia blossoms, mint juleps, and the Old South. In its bolder moments of elation it fancies itself the blueblood of bluebloods, though in introspective periods of depression it must recognize that many a furtive gene from bushwhackers, hillbillies, and occasionally from Shanty Irish has fertilized the esoteric germ plasm of the slaveholders before reaching its present tenants. Here and there in the greenest pastures affluent industrialists from the North have purchased the choicest estates and surrounded by the varnished and polished mansions of the agrarian aristocracy relax from the harried competition of the market place. They raise blooded race horses, white faced cattle, and indulge themselves as country gentlemen. In short, the county seat mind like its dwelling has a white pillared façade to give it an antique quality but is freshly furnished with all the latest in technology. In addition, they find their conspicuous country living a helpful item in an era of high income taxes, for on their estates they may spend and spend and lose and lose what would have otherwise fallen into the hands of "that man in Washington," whether the class traitor from Hyde Park or the nobody from Independence, Missouri. In general these emulators of the landed gentry lack the amplitude of noble motive, or the generous *noblesse oblige* of a genuine Burkian aristocracy. The ethics of the market place lurk in its inner conscience. It is not incapable of a *beau geste* in a community chest drive or at a charity bazaar, but it is careful to keep its assessments low and thereby contributes to low standards of schools and other public services. It is not consciously hard-hearted; it merely lives somewhat aloof.

Though of the country, the county seat elite is strangely astray from the country people. Their language and early habits distinguish them. Both have breakfast but the farmer has dinner at noon while the elite lunches and in the evening dines when the farmer has supper. This line of distinction is of great importance in social *savoir faire*, and many a county high school boy or girl has suffered great embarrassment in his failure to value the distinction.

Sometimes the dirt farmers break out in revolt against the domination of the county seat and elect one of their members to be sheriff or county judge, but soon the newly chosen ones are absorbed into the county seat governing class mores. Generally, the county seat and its politically conscious courthouse officers control politics by the process of influence percolating down to the substratum of small farmers and tenants. The humbler element seeks overtly the advice of their betters partly from inertia and partly hoping to gain from the subtle flattery of giving their landlords and merchant neighbors the feeling of being politically important. Accordingly, the elite instinctively dislikes any politician who injects issues which arouse the farmers to independence or consciousness of self-interest opposed to its leaders. Where poll taxes or literacy tests exist they are helpful to the elite in maintaining its position. The leaders control the election process and thereby keep political and economic power alike in their own hands. In this fashion they keep assessments down, tax rates fixed, and the schools in proper hands. The churches likewise, if any revolt were possible, are always mindful of the real location of sovereignty.

Like all elites, that of the county seat rarely examines its inarticulate major premises. Its values are accepted because they are so self-evident. Neither beneficiaries nor victims question the immutability nor the righteousness of their standards. Prescriptive right is the unwritten law which covers their governance. For this reason race or labor "agitators" are regarded as literally "agitators," for they question or attack values which have been set for three or four generations in the hard concrete of custom. The response to embarrassing inquiries is an inarticulate wrath not unlike the rage of the Roosevelt haters in industrial regions whose right to govern, whose fundamental ethic was questioned by Franklin D. Roosevelt.

The southern governing class tended to accept Roosevelt because they were in difficult times in 1933, and his attacks upon Tories and Big Business did not hurt them, but fitted into their patterns of traditional antagonism to industry. When it began to appear that "forgotten men" included Negroes and white sharecroppers, their suspicions were aroused. They wanted to dismiss it all as a vote-getting scheme up north. The formation of sharecroppers' unions and the appearance of live labor organizers in textile communities roused their ire, part of which was displaced upon the purge attempt of 1938.

The coming of war tended to dissipate this bitterness, and mutual prosperity lessened the feelings which had begun to rise locally. The county seat has never fared better in its history than from 1941 to 1947. Prices of cotton and tobacco rose to phenomenal heights. The presence of lockers outside the control of the Office of Price Administration made meat rationing less burdensome than for urban dwellers. There was some grumbling about the sugar shortage, but otherwise they held a special position as farmers, for most of the county seat elite could claim special privileges for gasoline and tires in order to supervise their landholdings. After all, their kind operated the ration boards and understood the necessities of the situation perfectly.

The group was troubled somewhat by the reiteration of war aims about racial equality which emanated from high authority, but most irritating were the speeches of Vice-President Wallace. As the elegant squire of Hyde Park, Roosevelt was a symbol the pseudo-landed gentry appreciated, whereas Wallace was mid-western and looked terribly unlike a model gentleman, the secret admiration of the county seat elite, particularly the female part of it. Wallace's emphasis upon the "common man" and his overt appeals to Negroes roused the elite to such bitterness that it joined with the urban machines to unhorse him and nominate Truman in 1944. Truman, as a county seat Missourian, and former county judge, and the greatly advertised rebel views of his aged mother suited the county seat elite much better than the Iowa Robespierre. When Roosevelt died they breathed a sigh of relief, for this to them spelled the end of "Eleanor Clubs" and similar unpleasantness. They hoped politics like business would be as usual in the postwar South. The fact that Truman kept repeating the Roosevelt liberal utterances was not too disturbing for they felt confident he was doing it only to get votes. They grew more and more angry as it appeared he meant what he said, for this was egregious evidence of betrayal within their own clan not unlike that of Roosevelt to his. However, it was more difficult to forgive Truman, for not by the remotest chance could anyone regard him as a fine gentleman like Roosevelt. He was too blunt, too much a come-upper to have any snob appeal to the superior prejudices of the southern elite.

As the presidential election of 1948 approaches, the elite of county seatdom are ill at ease for they feel betrayed in their own household by one of their own kind, and most of all by their own political church, the Democratic party. Here and there an uneasy eye is cast in the direction of the

Republican party and Senator Taft. For like all governing classes the grossest treason is even the imagination of its own demise. The elite of the county seat has become highly specialized in its own privileges and lacks both flexibility of temperament and boldness of imagination. It might be said of it as Brooks Adams wrote of its industrial prototype:

> Neither capitalists nor lawyers are necessarily, or even probably, other than conscientious men. What they do is to think with specialized minds. All dominant types have been more or less specialized, if none so much as this, and this specialization has caused, as I understand it, that obtuseness of perception which has been their ruin when the environment which favored them has changed. All that is remarkable about the modern capitalist is the excess of his eccentricity, or his deviation from that resultant of forces to which he must conform. To us, however, at present, neither the morality nor the present mental eccentricity of the capitalist is so material as the possibility of his acquiring flexibility under pressure, for it would seem to be almost mathematically demonstrable that he will, in the near future, be subjected to a pressure under which he must develop flexibility or be eliminated.[9]

IV

THE SOUTH AND THE FUTURE OF THE DEMOCRATIC PARTY[1]

IT BOILS down to this: my fellow rascals are greedy plutocrats; yours are hill-billy democrats. Both hate the kind of democracy that we love, mine are greedy, yours are ignorant. I just happen to get more satisfaction fighting greed than ignorance—and I believe better results. Iowa and Kansas are more civilized than Mississippi and Georgia."[2]

We live in a period which we hope will be an era of reconstruction. Yet the dread shadow of atomic vaporization hangs menacingly over all of us as we try to rebuild an order out of the fragments after two decades of unparalleled frustration and tension in the midst of destruction and depression. The grim spectre of World War III which hovers about should lead us to a more precise examination of the issues in the forecast struggle. Is it a clash between the symbols of something called democracy and something called communism? If so, then what are the elements of the democratic way of life which are challenged? The reply is likely to be spontaneous and frequently unthinking. We have freedom; the Russians do not! Freedom to express a choice in our government, to dissent, to elect the "outs" to take the place of the "ins." But what is the true nature of these alternatives? How effective a choice do we have? Is it only a choice between the tweedledum Republicans and the tweedledee Democrats? Is it a real alternative or is it a choice between shadows without substance?

If we are about to engage in a gigantic world struggle which may see the end of us all, does it not behoove us to examine more minutely the nature of the party system, the choice, the freedom which we seek to export to Germany and Japan and enforce with the threat of utter destruction? How great a difference is there between the dualism of the Anglo-American party system and what the late and relatively unlamented Mussolini was wont to call the "monolithic" front of Fascism or the totalitarianism of Communism?

Freedom to dissent is meaningless unless it can express itself without restraint in public assembly and through action in cooperation with persons who hold similiar views. These organizations become political parties. The requirement of a majority for the election of candidates makes it almost imperative that no more than two parties exist in the United States. Likewise, the majority requirement forces the coalition of many diverse interests. Coalitions in the United States take place in national nominating conventions instead of in national parliaments as on the continent of Europe.

I am well aware, of course, that the point of view which I represent is by no means a unanimous one. There is a school of thought which holds that instead of offering two distinct and sharply different programs of action between which reason may choose, that the issues between our parties should be deliberately confused—left "fuzzy" is the expressive slang phrase for it. Proponents of this view argue that, if the differences between the two parties become too great, the loser in a hotly contested election which goes to fundamental issues will not accept peaceably the outcome of a ballot count. These people argue correctly that there must be substantial unanimity in accepting an election as the proper procedure for determining policy and selecting leadership. They point out the unwillingness of the Right to accept the vote in Spain in 1936 and consequently the resort to force and the arise of Spanish Fascism. Granting the force of this argument, one may well counter that Spain was not yet accustomed to the party process as a way of doing things.

Probably a better example is the peaceable acceptance

of the 1945 Labour victory in England by Winston Churchill and the Conservatives. Churchill has set a magnificent example of patriotism by leading His Majesty's loyal opposition and by pointing to weaknesses in the Labour program. He has served his nation and his party well. In similar fashion, Wendell Willkie's cheerful acquiescence in the precedent-smashing third term election of 1940 served to strengthen the processes of majority rule.

I cannot believe there is substantial danger of the issues reaching the violence point in America. It is true that political democracy and majority rule would be put to an acid test in a contest between, say, the Communist party with a program of complete abolition of private property and the Republican party as represented by its Old Guard. After all, both groups would have to appeal to a large body of middle class voters and each would have to modify its program to make this appeal.

For the proper education of voters, it is essential that issues should be rather fundamental. Such matters stir people to a reassessment of their values and to the belief that their thoughts and actions are important and worthwhile. I cannot imagine anything more likely to win a considerable following to extreme Communism than the deeply implanted belief on the part of large numbers of people that there is no peaceful way out. Such beliefs are the breeding ground for violent revolutions.

In a large country such as the United States the necessity of a majority and the existence of two parties make it extremely difficult for either party to have principles of internal consistency or coherence. Each party becomes a federation of local interests bound together by the cohesive power of public patronage, if not of public plunder. Accordingly, there is a constant internal warfare for control of the organization of each party to determine which of its minorities will control the power or sovereignty of the party. Because of the multiplicity of interests, the Republican party may welcome a Taft and a Morse, a Bricker and a Stassen, and the Democrats may have under the same shield, Wagner of New York and Bilbo of Mississippi, a Byrd of Virginia and a Taylor of Idaho. The control of the "organization" or party machinery carries with it the right to manipulate the party name and symbols, including the tremendous advantage of using the party tradition for purposes of inner party strategy. We know, of course, that American parties have become primarily names inlaid in a mosaic of nebulous traditions. The vast mass of voters are inert and vote under the party symbol generation after generation regardless of issues or of personalities. Moreover, the relative equality of the numbers adhering to the two party names makes it possible for any one of the numerous alert minorities to secede and threaten party victory by its desertion to the historic foe. It is the continual battle among these minorities for control of the party machinery which enlivens all party activity.

Historically, our party evolution began with the effort of an elite of New England and New York merchants and incipient industrialists combining with the southern colonial tidewater aristocracy to dominate the new republic under the Hamiltonian conception of aristocratic government. Jefferson and his Piedmont landed gentry together with frontier farmers and a small urban artisan class formed the opposition which eventually came to power through the inevitable majority of farmers in the South and West. This combination of farmers and workers was even more thoroughly cemented by the leadership of Andrew Jackson.

Gradually the tidewater slaveholding elite transferred its allegiance and control to the Democratic party. By the late 1850's it had full mastery. In 1844, this elite enforced its control on the Democratic party by the famous two-thirds rule, a device used to defeat Van Buren, who opposed the annexation of Texas and the expansion of a slaveholding agrarian imperialism. Under those circumstances both parties cracked, with the industrial wing of the Whig party annexing the wheat and corn farmers of the Middle West and the frontier into the newly formed Republican party. The whole party system crumbled, for the slaveholding landed gentry refused to abide by the rule of party government, the acceptance of the majority vote, or plurality vote in this case, and revolution followed.[3]

The new alliance of eastern business or industry and western farmers, under the name of the Republican party, governed the United States for all practical purposes from 1860 to 1933. For a generation the new governing class of big businessmen unified the economy of the country by means of a protective tariff and credit centralization under a battle cry of laissez faire, shielded by the bewhiskered façade of war veterans of the Grand Army of the Republic. Midwestern generals Grant, Hayes, Garfield, Harrison, and Major McKinley were the vote-catching devices used to capture the masses. A single defection to nonveteran Blaine of Maine in 1884 resulted in defeat, but at no time did the Democrats have complete control of the executive, both houses of the legislature, and the Supreme Court. That Grover Cleveland was not too greatly different from his Republican predecessors and successors was evidenced by his discovery of government by judicial injunction in the railway strikes. This political invention has proved its effectiveness in marshalling the symbols of sovereignty behind the propertied elite in the hands of Cleveland's only legitimate presidential successor in the Democratic party, Harry Truman.

In the meantime, in the South the broken slaveholding governing class was succeeded by a combination of middle-class farmers, county seat bankers, absentee landlords, cotton factors, tobacco warehouse operators, retail merchants, and middlemen in general. This group established itself in the vacuum left by the old slaveholders after the failure of the scheme of the radical Republicans to use the emancipated slaves as a means of giving themselves and their big business allies a permanent control of the federal government—in other words, an assurance of a permanent Republican majority. Behind the myth of moonlight and magnolia and under the aura of the "Lost Cause" this new county seat landed gentry and business class took over effective control of the Democratic party in the South and by means of the one-third veto the naming of national candidates for office. "White supremacy" became the shibboleth of this new elite and racial hatred the emotional instrument for persuading poor farmers and hillbillies to sustain the governing class.

Occasionally the grim facts of poverty and low cotton and tobacco prices broke through this crust of cohesion and near revolution was on hand. In the 1880's the Grangers, and in the 1890's the Populists, were close to effecting a union of poor whites and Negroes into a cohesive majority.[4] The county seat elite persuaded the poor whites to accept constitutional revisions which presumably would disfranchise Negroes alone by requiring as a prerequisite to voting payment of poll taxes and the interpretation of the constitution to the satisfaction of the local election board, i.e., the county seat elite. Thus the efforts of Ben Tillman and Tom Watson failed. (The latter succumbed in his final years to racial phobia; indeed his experience offers a good case for psychiatric investigation.) Most important, however, is the fact that the huge base of the electoral pyramid had been removed from voting, sometimes as many as three-fourths of the potential voters being cut off.

In 1896 the effort of William Jennings Bryan to convert the Democratic party into the old Jacksonian combine of labor, farmers, and little businessmen went on the rocks.[5] Mark Hanna tightened even more closely the grip of big business upon the Republican party. The accident of assassination brought the first of the troublesome Roosevelts to the presidency and for a time it seemed that the western wing of the Republican party might gain control, but the first Roosevelt was no more fortunate in his choice of a successor than the second. Accordingly, in 1912 the restive farmers and uneasy small townsfolk with Theodore Roosevelt marched unsuccessfully to Armageddon as Woodrow Wilson led his minority to power for an assault on credit, transportation, and business monopoly.[6] He had scarcely started until he was diverted into the first World War and the wisdom of Boise Penrose in holding on to the "organization" of the Republican party was vindicated. The Penrose candidate, Warren Harding, with his slogan of "Less government in business and more business in government" established in 1920 a prototype for reactionaries in 1948.

Successive defeats came to the Democrats, really the southern rump of the party, which vetoed Alfred E. Smith in 1924 and deserted him in 1928. A callow instructor in political science on November 7, 1928, with all the foresight of his "science" preached the funeral oration of the Democratic party. Reinforced by magazine articles by Walter Lippmann, and saturated in the learning of the *Nation* and *New Republic*, the prescient young political scientist pointed out that the Democratic party was hopelessly divided, because the eastern Democrats were urban, Catholic, wet, recent immigrants, and Tammany-ridden, whereas the southern wing was rural, Protestant, dry, old American, Anglo-Saxon, Ku Klux, and isolated in small towns. Four years from that date, after substantially recapturing Congress in 1930, the Democrats were celebrating the greatest victory in their history, the first real majority vote of the electorate they had received since 1856 with James Buchanan. Then it happened again, again, and yet again! For sixteen years both houses of Congress were Democratic and Roosevelt smashed his opposition four times. Thus the Democrats have known the longest period of uninterrupted party ascendancy since James Monroe.

In the first and second Agricultural Adjustment Acts and the Wagner Labor Relations Act the farmer-labor nature of the New Deal fusion was clearly revealed. The old

Jacksonian combination was at work again, but big business fell back to its formerly impregnable redoubt, the Supreme Court. After having triumphed in 1936, with the aid of John L. Lewis and the recently formed Committee for Industrial Organization, President Roosevelt faced up to the Supreme Court issue at the same time that an epidemic of "sit down" strikes hit the automobile factories, the heart of modern industrial America. The Supreme Court fight revealed clearly the decisive role of the courts in the question of majority collective rights versus minority property rights. The struggle opened great fissures in the Democratic party. In 1932, in order to hurdle the two-thirds rule, James A. Farley, for Roosevelt, had compromised with McAdoo and accepted John Nance Garner, Texas small town banker and sales tax advocate, as Roosevelt's running mate.[7] Along with him, apparently came Jesse Jones. The sit-down strikes were too much for Garner and the Supreme Court reform too much for Senators George, "Cotton" Ed Smith, Byrd, Glass, Tydings, Connally, and Bennett Clark, as well as some of the personally dissatisfied western Democrats like Burton Wheeler and Pat McCarran. Joe Robinson, majority floor leader in the Senate, had his fight won when death struck him down and left the Senate leaderless and the celebrated "Dear Alben" letter emerged. By a margin of one vote, ironically enough cast by "the man" Bilbo, who, perhaps, remembered his $6,500 job as a paper clipper with idealistic Henry Wallace in 1933, Barkley was chosen to succeed Robinson. Bilbo's unabiding hatred of Pat Harrison, his Mississippi colleague, who was Barkley's opponent, helped the Border state middle-of-the-roader win the leadership. From that day, the party internecine war was on.

In 1938 the southern conservatives set about to "purge" Barkley and in the ensuing fight Roosevelt campaigned actively against George, Tydings, and Smith. He was unsuccessful in all three fights, in no small measure, because Jim Farley and his "organization" did not set to work in a systematic fashion to break the sitting Senators.[8] Farley had, however, in 1936 demolished the one-third veto and thereby, perhaps, made possible the first third-term nomination in 1940. The breach in the Democratic party between the eastern and industrial wing, primarily labor, and the southern wing, primarily agrarian, led by the county seat elite, has never healed. From that date until April 12, 1945, it was a question of the succession to leadership in the "organization," a leadership which would control and manipulate the symbols of the party.

The battle for the Supreme Court was at last nominally won by Roosevelt. As reconstituted, the principal minorities are now perhaps proportionately represented on the court: the Catholic Church, one; the Jews, and Harvard, one; the Ku Klux Klan, one; New York State, one; the Pacific Northwest and Yale, one; Ohio Republicans, one; and Kentucky, three! The court has reinterpreted the commerce clause in such fashion that Congress now has the constitutional power to govern. The Wagner Act, AAA, and TVA are now constitutional but the story has not been completely told. The untimely death of Chief Justice Harlan F. Stone gave President Harry S. Truman an opportunity to place squarely in the center of a feuding court a nominal New Dealer, Fred M. Vinson, whose antecedents indicate him to be something else. The use of the injunction to break John L. Lewis's coal strike suggests that a new majority willing to manipulate the symbols of sovereignty on behalf of property again may have arisen. Further tests, particularly the application of the constitution to the Taft-Hartley Act, will reveal more clearly how effective this new group may be.

Big business was finally forced to its last bastion of defense, its position of remote control of the Democratic party. Roosevelt was not immortal. Short shrift was made of Wendell Willkie and his efforts to liberalize the Republican party. Railroads and utility companies as well as banks have long manifested an interest in the South. This interest has frequently shown itself in very positive ways in political campaigns.[9] This has happened in the Talmadge campaigns in Georgia, for example, and in support of Senator George in 1938. Likewise, the "Big Mule" is well known in Alabama.

The fight for control of the Democratic party organization, I assume, was a major factor in the Jesse Jones—Henry Wallace struggle in 1943.[10] As Wallace shifted more and more from the position of a Middle Western agrarian, and no longer thought of a farm problem, but principally of a consumption problem with full employment in industry as the clue to prosperity for farmers, the effort to eliminate Wallace as crown prince grew more intensive. Opposition to a fourth term centered in Texas where the possibility of voting for a third candidate was presented as a device to prevent Roosevelt's re-election and to develop the bargaining weapon for defeating Wallace for the Vice-Presidency. The South as represented by the Byrds, Joneses, Georges, McKellars, *et al.*, preferred a Throttlebottom to Wallace, and Throttlebottom they got. How Wallace was defeated is a matter of history.[11] By and large it was the big city machines (whose leaders resent competitive trade union machines) and the county seat elite that pulled the trick. There were some cracks in the southern leadership, notably Pepper of Florida and Arnall of Georgia, and persistent rumor has it that Barkley intended to throw his weight behind Wallace on the next ballot (which never took place).

There are many things we don't know yet, and one is whether the conflict between Russia and the United States had begun to sharpen up before Roosevelt's death, but historians of a speculative turn of mind, if we have any future history to write, may turn inquisitive eyes upon what difference it would have made in world history if Henry Wallace instead of the best county judge Jackson County, Missouri ever had, had been president in those fateful years between

1945 and 1948. Enough has been said to indicate clearly the significance of the South and its role in the Democratic party to lend interest to a more intensive analysis.

In his *Education*, Henry Adams has mordantly referred to Yankee politics in these words:

> Politics, as a practice, whatever its profession, had always been the systematic organization of hatreds, and Massachusetts politics had been as harsh as the climate. The chief charm of New England was harshness of contrasts and extremes of sensibility—a cold that froze the blood, and a heat that boiled it—so that the pleasure of hating—one's self if no better victim offered—was not its rarest amusement. . . . .[12]

Southerners have never had to resort to such introspective and puritanical hatreds. The list of southern hatreds extends from the Abolitionists (including William Lloyd Garrison and Mrs. Harriet Beecher Stowe) and the Radical Republicans (especially Charles Sumner and Thaddeus Stevens, the latter Hollywoodized in "The Birth of a Nation") down to Henry Wallace and John L. Lewis. Hatred was organized in that great pre-Nazi body, the Ku Klux Klan. For three-quarters of a century the South has evidenced all the characteristics of the psychosis of defeat. If anyone is an optimist over the prospects of our policies of reconstruction in Germany and Japan he might well study the story of reconstruction in the South. Partly as a result of accident and partly as the consequence of the peculiar natural resources of the South, its economy became even more wedded to cotton and tobacco after the Civil War than before. Livestock production declined and any inclination towards industry was likely to be regarded as a betrayal of the "Lost Cause." Free labor was not accepted after the Civil War any more than before. The sharecropper-land tenure system maximizes feudalism and minimizes free labor. I think I am safe in saying that the governing class of southern county seats has not yet accepted the Thirteenth Amendment. The governing class has bitterly resisted all efforts of labor to organize sharecroppers. Some people may recall that a minister of the gospel was horsewhipped and a woman run out of the county when they sought to unionize sharecroppers in Arkansas a decade ago.

It is little wonder that Eugene Cox of Georgia and John Rankin of Mississippi are two of the foremost opponents of organized labor in Congress. As a matter of fact, the whole committee system with its custom of seniority rule has strengthened the power of the county seat governing class beyond its voting power. All students of Congress are aware of the fact that the seniority, or senility rule, if you prefer, has fostered the power of the one-party system. Without fear of defeat in the ordinary pendulum swings of politics, some southern politicians can rise to committee chairmanships, and can there effectively block the action of a Democratic president, the leader of his party, who must create and sell to the national electorate a program of economic and social action.

We are now brought to the heart of our central problem. The economy of the South, together with its traditional developments, has created a governing class which has disfranchised its political opposition and thereby effectively placed itself in the saddle of the Democratic party. This party historically and institutionally should be the alternative to the Republican party. It cannot offer this alternative as long as the seniority rule in Congress and its own control in local districts is kept impregnable. With unerring accuracy Ilya Ehrenburg, the Soviet journalist in his articles in *Pravda* in 1946, picked the South as the Achilles' heel of American democracy.[13] The treatment of both labor and Negro minorities in this region belies our protestations of freedom, liberty, and political democracy, to say nothing of social or economic democracy. Franklin Roosevelt may have made the executive, the legislative, and even the Supreme Court more responsive to popular control, but he failed in his attempt to democratize the Democratic party.

He failed to leave either a reasonable alternative organization to the one dominated by big business, or anything but a feeble and lukewarm leadership in the executive.

The political influence of the South is by no means confined to the Democratic party. The existence of a Republican party in the South which is scarcely more than a shell, composed of pliable if not purchasable officeholders, discourages the more liberal element nationally in the party. There is small doubt that the great majority of Republican voters wanted Theodore Roosevelt to be their presidential nominee in 1912. This was shown by the number of delegates he won in presidential preference primaries and by the fact that he received a million more votes in the final election than the regular Republican nominee, Taft. Yet control of the southern delegates made it possible for Penrose to retain the organization of the party and for Taft to dictate his own renomination. The southern delegates played no small part in the choice of Harding in 1920 and many persons will recall C. Bascom Slemp and Calvin Coolidge in 1924.[14] In other words, the elements in the Republican party led by Wayne Morse, Aiken, and Flanders, which would like to lessen the grip of big business upon the party, are handicapped by the unrepresentative and patronage-seeking group of Republicans from southern states where, under present conditions, they have not a ghost of a chance to win an election. If the interest of the South as a section, or as a region, is in freeing itself from eastern industrial control, certainly one of the places to begin is in ridding the nation of a system under the rules of which both parties are overbalanced in favor of enemies of a developing welfare of the masses of the southern people.

No accurate student of public affairs can honestly say that either big business or the Republican party created this peculiar situation in the South and the Democratic party, but certainly both profit from it and do little to try to eliminate the conditions making for it. As long as the

South continues to represent an illiberal rump of the Democratic donkey just so long will northern liberals and industrial labor feel reluctant to join with the party. The Rankins, Coxes, Talmadges, and their kind can always be trotted out to frighten off those who do not approve of Republican leadership or policies but who might otherwise be persuaded to join the Democrats. Labor has the largest group of organized voters in the country. The Negroes present a marginal group of voters in many states like New York, Pennsylvania, Ohio, and Illinois. Their enthusiasm can never be great for a party which through the seniority rule brings a man of Bilbo's character to the chairmanship of the Senatorial District of Columbia Committee, to be "Mayor of Washington,"—when over a third of the population of Washington is Negro.

There are, accordingly, very explosive possibilities in the South in prospect for the next decade. First of all, cotton in the Southeast is sick nigh unto death. The price of cotton, and of tobacco too, for that matter, has been pushed up by governmental action far beyond what the world market will sustain. In the meantime, not only have competitive areas outside the United States gone into cotton production, but likewise the Southwest and southern California. Cotton production in these new regions is either already highly mechanized or can be easily converted to mechanization. Add to this the very likely prospect of the introduction of the cotton picker into the whole cotton economy and we may have a technological revolution of as serious import as that following the introduction of the cotton gin itself.

The 1943–1947 *Yearbook of Agriculture* declares:

> Some segments of American agriculture are still relatively untouched by mechanization, notably cotton and tobacco in the Southeastern States. But mechanization of cotton production in the South is not far off. The use of tractor power is likely to be followed by machine cultivation and harvesting of cotton. In the next few years perhaps some progress will be made in adapting machinery to tobacco production.[15]

The displacement of one or two millions of sharecroppers, both black and white, might bring consequences of not only national but world-wide significance. The movement of the "Okies" and "Arkies" to the Pacific Coast so trenchantly presented in John Steinbeck's *The Grapes of Wrath* may have been only a foretaste of things to come.[16] If these displaced farmer-workers turn to northern and eastern cities seeking industrial employment, what will be the result of their impact upon unions and urban housing? If northern and eastern industry in the name of decentralization should seek to move to the South in order to get the benefits of docile Anglo-Saxon labor, what will be the results for real estate values and welfare programs in present industrial areas? May not the presence of a wage-cutting Negro minority excite a nation-wide racial hatred which may be mobilized by some future Hitler or Huey Long as a scapegoat for the frustrations of an industrial age? Already the Ku Klux Klan revival and the presence of other racial-hatred propagandists have sent meteors of fear across our political skies. Whether these more dramatic events take place or not, it is clear that the increased productivity of agriculture during the war and the necessity of retiring many areas of depleted soils to grass have their own portent. A livestock-grass economy may produce an enclosure movement in the South, and elsewhere for that matter, with economic and political consequences nearly equal to those of the introduction of sheep farming into feudal England.[17] All of these are matters of national import and must be treated nationally.

Already organized labor has dimly realized the meaning of these potential developments and is seeking to organize southern labor. Is it any wonder that the southern wing of the Democratic party gave President Truman little help in his effort to prevent big business from putting across the Taft-Hartley bill? To cripple labor at the genesis of its drive in the South would be very helpful to the southern governing class in controlling the new industrial South. In 1946, when I inquired of a southern labor organization leader if the southern police were opposing the new drive with violence, he smiled and replied affirmatively. "But," he went on, "this doesn't give us too much trouble. Of 175 organizers, 157 are ex-G.I.'s. They know how to take care of themselves. If one can't do the job we send in six or seven." The battle of Athens, Tennessee, revealed how well the former soldiers remembered their training.[18] It likewise showed up clearly the nature and power of the county seat governing class. Perhaps this new revelation was unnecessary as the testimony in the investigation of Harlan County, Kentucky, was eloquent in this regard.[19]

It is needless for me to dwell at length upon the significance of race for politics local, national, and international. In 1908 Graham Wallas in his *Human Nature in Politics* wrote:

.... The fight for democracy in Europe and America during the eighteenth and early nineteenth centuries was carried on by men who were thinking only of the European races..... The ordinary man now finds that the sovereign vote has (with exceptions numerically insignificant) been in fact confined to nations of European origin. But there is nothing in the form or history of the representative principle which seems to justify this, or to suggest any alternative for the vote as a basis of government. Nor can he draw any intelligible and consistent conclusion from the practice of democratic States in giving or refusing the vote to their non-European subjects. The United States, for instance, have silently and almost unanimously dropped the experiment of negro suffrage. In that case, owing to the wide intellectual gulf between the West African negro and the white man from northwest Europe, the problem was comparatively simple; but no serious attempt has yet been made at a new solution of it, and the Americans have been obviously puzzled in dealing with the more subtle racial questions created by the immigration of Chinese and Japanese and Slavs, or by the government of the mixed populations in the Philippines.[20]

Race hatred was the demagogic base for the foundation of Nazism. Class hatred is the emotional base for the communist dictatorship. Both of these problems are at the heart of the crisis in the Democratic party in the nation and in the South. Philosophers who proclaim the democratic way of life believe reason must find the way to the solution of social and economic questions. Reason must choose between alternatives; the party system must offer those alternatives. If, in 1948, the voters have only the choice between a Republican Taft or Bricker and a Democratic Truman or Byrd, then the party process has failed in its function of presenting alternatives. Freedom ceases to be freedom when there are no effective choices left. Voters deserve better than to have two Republican parties as they did in 1924, for example. If capitalism is simply a two-headed giant or a Janus-faced god, then its defense against monolithic totalitarianism either of class or race will be weakened, if not destroyed.

One need not go all the way with Sigmund Neumann[21] or Peter Drucker[22] about the nature of mass or industrial society, but he must accept the point of view that our future is industrial and that we must find new freedoms in social and industrial organizations or the traditional freedoms coming from our agrarian and frontier heritage will perish from the earth.

"No man is really free unless he can tell his boss to go to hell, and then get a job somewhere else; no society is truly free if one authority makes all the important decisions."[23] This statement of John Fischer's is vital to a free people. Neither capitalism nor communism offers that freedom now nor in the foreseeable future. Even college professors can testify to this, though the present "bull" market in professors is helpful. Two ways point to a popular control of our future industrial order. One of these is offered by the British Labour party; the other by the Communist party. The first is within the democratic tradition of majority choice with protection of minority rights. The other is not. Insofar as the masses of industrial workers feel they can make a choice in the gradual evolution towards popular control they will likely maintain the present procedure of gradual evolution, but if this avenue of choice is cut off they may be forced to try other devices; whether successfully or not is another story.

In other words, the problem of the South is the problem of the nation and the problem of the world, the introduction of reason into the issues of race and class. If political invention can find a way of making the democratic process effective in the South it will have perfected a political technology which may be of use throughout the world.

Since the Civil War the Democratic party has become a kind of crisis party. When big business domination of the Republican party becomes too bad, the public turns to the Democratic party for relief. The more successful the Democratic party is with its program in offering immediate relief the sooner it is turned from power. When the country is prosperous it votes Republican; when it is sick it votes Democratic. If the Democratic party can offer no other medicine than that offered by the Republicans, then voters have no hope of any change or any improvement.

The tragic fact for the Democratic party today is that when it loses strength in the North and West, it loses its liberal leadership and becomes, because of conservative southern control, more and more like the Republican party. Then fewer and fewer northern and western voters have the urge to vote for it as an alternative. As long as the Democratic party fails to afford an outlet for the millions of southern disinherited, its sharecroppers and workers, black and white, it occupies the position in the South of the Republican party in the North. It is a conservative elite dedicated to the preservation of the property system as it is, an institution devoted to preserving what is, rather than an agency seeking new roads for peaceful and gradual transition to the future. If the Democratic party is to serve a useful role in the society of the future it must serve as an instrument of change.

Technology is the real revolutionist. The physicists are far more dangerous to the *status quo* than the political scientists. The transition must be made. The opportunity of the Democratic party is in helping to make the gradual evolution. That, I take it for granted, was the aim and purpose of Franklin D. Roosevelt, who sought to weld together a cohesive body of support for a party of progressive social change. That he failed to make the Democratic party into such an instrument is probably his most notable failure. In other respects, he was the most effective political leader American politics has produced. It is ironic that he should have so significantly failed in altering the instrument which helped him to power.

If I have succeeded in sharpening up the patent fact that the South is in the strategic center of the future of the Democratic party, and if I have made plainer what should be a self-evident fact that the value of a two party system is in its effectiveness in making freedom real, thereby offering a propaganda of the deed to offset the propaganda of the word put forth by competing ideologies which regard political democracy as a sham, I am content. The best way to disprove such propaganda is to make democracy and freedom vital.

V

SOUTHERN POLITICS IN AN ATOMIC AGE: A CREATIVE FUTURE?

THE somewhat flamboyant title of this last discussion is meant to raise questions rather than to give final answers. Most of us are probably familiar enough with the term "Atomic Age." Personally, I should like to forget the term and the fact, even as I would like to forget death and income taxes. Unfortunately the splitting of the atom has robbed victory of its sweetness and equalized victor, ally, and vanquished in awe and fear before the new forces unleashed by the cunning of man. In its presence we stand paralyzed and terrorized. I belong to a lost generation which separates two other lost generations. My older schoolmates marched off to war "to make the world safe for democracy," as I was painfully emerging from short trousers. My students were taken off to "a war of survival" as the hairs on my head grew fewer and while the lingering ones were whitening with the passing years. At the same time, my physique was becoming less and less military in aspect or usefulness. Accordingly, I have stood isolated on a little hillock of time where I could watch my predecessors and successors rush into the valleys of destruction. "Theirs not to reason why, Theirs but to do and die."

Already I am wondering whether I am "educating" another generation with a rendezvous with destiny or with disaster. It is no idle dream or nightmare to speculate whether ours is the last generation. "But what does this have to do with southern politics?" you may ask. The answer is: everything. In the preceding chapter we indicated that the two great problems our time has to overcome are the hatreds of race and the antagonisms of capital and labor. In the South we have in miniature the problems of the world. The generally assumed curses of racial minorities and poverty pose the greatest challenges to the ingenuity of man. If the South can develop a political inventiveness which can approach answers to these thorny issues, the world and all future mankind will be its eternal debtors. Our burdens are our opportunities. It behooves us to rise to the need. This is a challenge to southern politics but no less one to southern social science, and for that matter to southern religion.

Someway, somehow, we must make the transition from the politics of hatred to the politics of affection; we must move from the politics of aggression and frustration to the politics of integration and unity. It is easier to raise the questions than to answer them; it is easier to exhort than it is to act, but somewhere and sometime we must start. Inertia is the chief enemy. The philosophy of quietism, of "not sticking out one's neck," of social and political aloofness, is almost as sterile and defeating as hatred itself. The cynics who believe man is hopeless and the Calvinists who damn him with original sin do equally little to help in our quandary. For example, this view of man may be illuminating but not too helpful:

> I desire to contemplate him from this point of view—this premise: that he was not made for any useful purpose, for the reason that he hasn't served any; that he was most likely not even made *intentionally*; and that his working himself up out of the oyster bed to his present position was probably a matter of surprise and regret to the Creator . . . . . For his history, in all climes, all ages and all circumstances, furnishes oceans and continents of proof that of all the creatures that were made he is the most detestable. Of the entire brood he is the only one—the solitary one—that possesses malice.
>
> That is the basest of all instincts, passions, vices—the most hateful. That one thing puts him below the rats, the grubs, the trichinae. He is the only creature that inflicts pain for sport, knowing it to *be* pain. But if the cat knows she is in-

flicting pain when she plays with the frightened mouse, then we must make an exception here; we must grant that in one detail man is the moral peer of the cat. *All* creatures kill—there seems to be no exception; but of the whole list, man is the only one that kills for fun; he is the only one that kills in malice, the only one that kills for revenge. Also—in all the list he is the only creature that has a nasty mind.[1]

This statement comes from the pen of Mark Twain. While it may be a trenchant indictment it does not help us for the future. Under the circumstances, we have to turn to science and to tradition if they are not mutually exclusive and I do not think they are.

The first of these is tradition, the western European Judeo-Christian tradition of the brotherhood of man, though a great debt is owed to the Stoic conception derived from Hellenism. Stoicism was the philosophic foundation stone of Roman law and ultimately the invigorating principle of the Roman Empire. Whether we go towards the Pax Americana of Mr. Henry Luce's dreams or to world federation, the ideological genesis of unity will need to be the likenesses of man, not his dissimilarities. The fact that all men are equally mortal, regardless of race or wealth, may be the necessary basis for ultimate action. A new appreciation of the functional necessity of all men and a forgetting of diversities, save as these differences enrich the cultural heritage of all of us, is fundamental.

The futility of the argument over whether men or women are superior should have been demonstrated long ago. Both are biologically necessary to the preservation of the species and the well-known limitations of males as mothers and females as fathers is irrelevant, immaterial, and irrational. Every diversity does not of itself imply a relationship of inequality or inferiority or of superiority. To argue whether the violin or the clarinet contributes more to the symphony is absurd. Both are essential. Both management and labor are essential to production; both colored and white are essential to the southern tradition and necessary to the enrichment of southern culture. It should be needless to point out that a Carver by his creative genius has immensely improved the lot of all southerners without regard to color, race, or caste, just as the voice of a Marian Anderson enriches the musical enjoyment of the whole nation. By the same token a poverty-stricken, disease-ridden "nigger town," "on the other side of the track," is a menace to the health and morals of the entire community. Germs and viruses are remarkably democratic. They know not class or race distinctions (though ultimately one people may develop relative immunity as the Negro has to hookworm and the white man less susceptibility to tuberculosis); the employer may contract the disease from the employee.

Fundamental to a new and creative conception of southern politics is the development of the idea that instead of fighting over the distribution of scarcity between blacks and whites, or workers and managers, we should be producing more to be distributed—more goods and more services. Adequate health services and adequate diet are fundamental to good health and good health is vital to an improved outlook upon life, to an attitude of good will towards one's fellows. The South must be less concerned about who is kept in his place and more concerned with how the place of all is raised. Our principal objective must be not to keep anybody down but to raise everybody up. The first requisite in the political education of the South is the rejection once and for all of each and every man who preaches the hatred of his fellow man. Hatred has become a luxury which will have to be dispensed with in an atomic world; we cannot afford it. I include in that group the purveyors of class hatred as well as the Roosevelt haters, some of whom have become professional.

All communities, organization-ridden as they are, need one more body whose purpose it is to kill rumors and vicious hatred spreading. This body should be a clearinghouse composed of both employers and employees and of both black and white. Its purpose should be the exposure of false accusations against any minority—or a majority either, for that matter. Both scientifically and ethically such an organization is justified and necessary. If possible, such bodies might eventually become public agencies with a positive program of generating good will. The South has had a surfeit of ill will. I do not mean just a wishy-washy saccharine kind of attitude. I mean an agency which will positively rejoice in the achievements of all people regardless of kind when a genuine accomplishment has been made.

If the South is to be more economically productive it will need to industrialize. That now seems to be a general aspiration though there are many who are reluctant to do so. I have been a member, and still belong to that group in some ways. I abhor an industrialization which is another name for exploitation of workers, for the destruction of beauty, for the creation of Ducktowns, for the introduction of new class distinctions between "cotton heads" and the middle class. But to increase what there is to be distributed, men must be given tools which will make them more productive. The doctrine of scarcity must go, the principle of the closed shop must be socialized whether it be in a carpenter's union where the wage rate per hour is the measure of union achievement, or whether it be in the utility executive's office where it is decided to raise rates and produce less, or whether it be in the medical association's curb on an increase in doctors. The principle of the closed shop and monopolized scarcity did not originate in unions; it has been a principle of business for generations. Monopolies and cartels and farmers' organizations as well must be persuaded to see that controlled scarcity is as bad when supported by business and farmers as when advanced by labor.

The production and distribution of plenty is a *sine qua non* to the dilution of hatred, to the dissipation of the politics of aggression and the promotion of the politics of integration and affection. Through the ages man has responded to the stimuli of fear, insecurity, and revenge. Possibly the atomic age offers the opportunity for the creation of plenty. An environment of abundance might offer stimuli to alter what we are prone to consider the unalterable nature of man. Fewer frustrations might mean fewer hatreds to be displaced upon psychological scapegoats, either minorities or majorities. Would it not be a tragic epitaph for man, to write of him: He died just when there was some hope for him? Might not the South be a laboratory for disproving once and for all the most defeatist of all pessimism, the cliché that human nature never changes? The lack of faith in man is the beginning of despair. For example, a petition to the Tennessee Constitutional Convention of 1870 included the following:

> We hold that the negro race is the lowest order of human beings, incapable in themselves of a virtuous, intelligent or free government; and for the truth of this, we appeal to history, and challenge the world to show a single exception.
>
> We hold that the inferiority of the negro to the white man, in race, color and capacity for permanent, well-ordered government, has been fixed by Him, who "doeth all things well," and whose natural or revealed law has never been violated by any human government without disaster and confusion. The proud Castilian violated this natural law, when, instead of recognizing in the body politic, the distinction which God had made between him and the Aztec, the Indian and the negro, he made them politically equal, and swift destruction came upon him, insomuch that his *pure* blood cannot now be traced in the mongrel, miscegenating horde, who, by never-ceasing revolution and civil strife, desolate the rich and beautiful lands of Mexico.[2]

Compare this impassioned statement with the temperate comment of Robert E. Lee: "My own opinion is that at this time they [Negroes] cannot vote intelligently and that giving them the right of suffrage would open the door to a good deal of demagogism and lead to embarrassments in various ways."[3]

Human behavior is the response of inner urges to the stimuli of environment. Behavior will be determined in no small measure by the nature of the stimuli to which man's nervous system is exposed. Modification of human behavior may follow alteration in the environment. It is fruitless to enter the controversy as to whether heredity or environment is the more important. Both are essential. We may agree with Graham Wallas that:

> One of the most fertile sources of error in modern political thinking consists, indeed, in the ascription to collective habit of that comparative permanence which only belongs to biological inheritance. A whole science can be based upon easy generalizations about Celts and Teutons, or about East and West, and the facts from which the generalizations are drawn may all disappear in a generation. National habits used to change slowly in the past, because new methods of life were seldom invented and only gradually introduced, and because the means of communicating ideas between man and man or nation and nation were extremely imperfect; so that a true statement about a national habit might, and probably would, remain true for centuries. But now an invention which may produce profound changes in social or industrial life is as likely to be taken up with enthusiasm in some country on the other side of the globe as in the place of its origin.[4]

If we move, in the South, from an environment of scarcity or poverty to one of relative abundance, then is it not reasonable to expect a lessening of hatred which is fundamentally based upon fear or insecurity? To make the transition from a primarily agrarian to a primarily industrial or technological society will require phenomenal efforts of training and education. As a professional in the latter field, with two decades of experience, I am not prone to overestimate the successes of education. I realize all too well the difficulties in changing blind spots and in modifying stereotypes. I am not as skeptical as one of my former colleagues who contends that no amount of education ever cured anybody of anti-Semitism. If I were convinced of the truth of that statement, I would immediately surrender my credentials and resume my interrupted career as a farmer. I do not underestimate the task. But I would approach it with hope. My point of view would be in the spirit of the following argument:

> By the "mud-sill" theory it is assumed that labor and education are incompatible, and any practical combination of them impossible. According to that theory, a blind horse upon a tread-mill is a perfect illustration of what a laborer should be—all the better for being blind, that he could not kick understandingly. According to that theory, the education of laborers is not only useless but pernicious and dangerous. In fact, it is, in some sort, deemed a misfortune that laborers should have heads at all. Those same heads are regarded as explosive materials, only to be safely kept in damp places, as far as possible from that peculiar sort of fire which ignites them. A Yankee who could invent a strong-handed man without a head would receive the everlasting gratitude of the "mud-sill" advocates.
>
> But free labor says, "No." Free labor argues that as the Author of man makes every individual with one head and one pair of hands, it was probably intended that heads and hands should cooperate as friends, and that that particular head should direct and control that pair of hands. As each man has one mouth to be fed, and one pair of hands to furnish food, it was probably intended that that particular pair of hands should feed that particular mouth—that each head is the natural guardian, director, and protector of the hands and mouth inseparably connected with it; and that being so, every head should be cultivated and improved by whatever will add to its capacity for performing its charge. In one word, free labor insists on universal education.[5]

The South, it has been estimated, will furnish over 50 per cent of the population of the nation by 1960. However unproductive the South may be in other respects it has not failed to produce a bountiful crop of children. To train this group of youngsters in the technological skills of an industrial civilization is a heavy and expensive task. It has been pointed out repeatedly that the expense of educating this human raw material is a great burden upon the South, especially in view of the fact that the finished product is exported during its most productive period to create wealth for other parts of the country. Some years ago I speculated

A CREATIVE FUTURE? 81

that ultimately the export of Democrats from the South would give a majority of Democrats to the nation sometime in the next generation. The exodus of "Okies" and "Arkies" to California and the migration of sharecroppers to Detroit certainly has had its influence, but a more profound examination led me to alter my conclusions, for it is from the most heavily Republican areas of the South, the Appalachian region, that the export of population is the heaviest. If this region continues to be one of the chief breeding grounds of the nation an irresistible Republican trend might fall upon us.

But to return to the main topic. It seems to me that it is only on the basis of adult training of the present population and the education of the young that we have any foundation or reason for optimism for the possible solution of the baffling difficulties of the disadvantaged classes of the South. Let us examine the situation of Mississippi. Almost one half of its population is colored. In fact, Mississippi is at the heart of our political problem, for in addition to a large and poor Negro population, there is a large body of ignorant and illiterate whites. It is but to repeat a truism of the research of recent years to say that if Mississippi spent her entire income upon education she could not meet her responsibilities. Her task is to bring a relatively primitive people, handicapped by the experience of their forebears under slavery, and a large number of retarded whites up to the requirements of a technological society both in skills and in attitudes. Mississippi needs not only sympathy, instead of universal condemnation, but something more substantial in the way of financial assistance. The path of statesmanship lies not in a holier-than-thou attitude on the part of the more fortunate parts of the nation, but in the recognition of a mutual responsibility. The introduction of the cotton picker may mean that Mississippi will export her problems to the nation, and possibly export hatred along with her surplus workers. Mississippi, on the other hand, must not insist that she can maintain an effective nullification of the Fourteenth and Fifteenth Amendments and a federal subsidy at the same time.

Though I have little personal faith in literacy tests for voting, I think that expediency may dictate a development of that kind. Let Mississippi substitute a reasonably attainable educational standard for its present indirect color barrier and then let the federal government with its funds aid as many people as possible to attain this standard. Suppose Mississippi were to repeal her present ingenious devices for disfranchising the Negroes and poor white voters and replace them with a single requirement for all, namely, that each registered voter should show legal evidence of completion of the fifth grade in school. Any other grade may be offered; I have no prejudice in favor of five. Immediately the burden is shifted to the voter to finish at least a minimum of schooling. He has an incentive to complete at least this much education. The cards are not completely stacked against him as they are at the present. This standard complies with the criterion of John Stuart Mill that good government includes the preparation of people for the next upward step in civilization.[6] The state of Mississippi and the United States could once more face the world without hypocrisy and truthfully say that political democracy in the South is not a sham and a fraud, for anyone who tries hard enough and has the ability may participate in elections, regardless of race, sex, creed, or previous condition of servitude. Mississippi could say to the nation, "We are doing our best with the money we have. Give us a grant-in-aid so we can do a better job." Even Senator Robert A. Taft has been convinced of the inability of Mississippi and other nonindustrial but heavily populated states to meet the minimum standards of financial support for a barely essential educational system. Setting up a reasonably attainable standard as here suggested would bring an end to federal anti–poll tax legislation, probably to federal antilynching legislation and in considerable measure to filibustering in the United States Senate.

I use Mississippi purposely, for the problem is more difficult in that state than in any other. First of all, Negroes compose 47.1 per cent of the potential voters of the state, the largest proportion of the potential electorate in any state. Furthermore, Negroes compose more than a majority of the possible electorate in 31 of Mississippi's 82 counties. As far as Negro majorities are concerned there are 150 counties, or 10 per cent of the 1,443 southern counties, which have a possible majority of colored voters. Ninety of these counties are to be found in the three states of Georgia (40), Mississippi

TABLE 2

COUNTIES WITH A MAJORITY OF POTENTIAL NEGRO VOTING POPULATION IN FIFTEEN SOUTHERN STATES[a]

Name of State	Number of Counties	Per Cent Negro of All Potential Voters	Number of Counties with Potential Negro Majority	Per Cent of All Counties with Potential Negro Majority
All states	1443	21.6	150	10.4
Alabama	67	33.4	15	22.4
Arkansas	75	24.6	9	12.0
Florida	67	25.5	2	3.0
Georgia	159	32.8	40	25.2
Kentucky	120	8.4	0	0.0
Louisiana	64	34.4	13	20.3
Maryland	23	15.5	0	0.0
Mississippi	82	47.1	31	37.8
Missouri	114	6.6	0	0.0
North Carolina	100	25.3	6	6.0
Oklahoma	77	7.1	0	0.0
South Carolina	46	38.7	19	41.3
Tennessee	95	18.1	2	2.1
Texas	254	14.0	4	1.6
Virginia	100	23.1	9	9.0

[a] Based on 1940 Census.

(31), and South Carolina (19). Of the remaining 50 counties, 15 are in Alabama and 13 in Louisiana. The latter state has already abolished the poll tax and uses other means, or "literacy" tests, to disfranchise. It may be pointed out that North Carolina, with six counties with potential Negro majorities, has long ago abolished the poll tax. In Florida, without a poll tax, two counties fall in the same classification. In only five states does the Negro represent approximately one-third or more of the possible voting population; Alabama with 33.4 per cent; Georgia, 32.8 per cent; Louisiana, 34.4 per cent; South Carolina, 38.7 per cent; and Mississippi, as we have seen, 47.1 per cent. The problem is less accentuated in Tennessee with only 18.1 per cent of its potential electorate colored and with only two counties of its 95 showing possible Negro majorities. The same situation is true in Texas where 14.0 per cent of the potential electorate is Negro and four of 254 counties have possible Negro majorities.

But if the South and the United States are going to take a positive attitude towards citizenship they will have to go further than the action already outlined. A gigantic effort for adult education must be undertaken immediately. This is necessary for two purposes. First of all, the prospect of industrialization and the introduction of mechanization into agriculture points to the end of the ignorant, illiterate, unskilled farm hand. It means the training of workers to be ever more productive. The cow demands more intelligence of her caretaker than does cotton. Along with industrialization in the South will come urbanization. Urbanization has already considerably modified the pattern of politics in the South as in the nation. A rotten borough system is in the making equal to that in England in the first decades of the nineteenth century. The situation in Georgia is the worst, for the county unit system in use there has rather effectively disfranchised thousands of city dwellers. Only in this fashion was Eugene Talmadge able to win the Democratic nomination for governor in 1946. The fact that there is a great movement of Negroes to the cities is part of the picture. Rural government will ultimately have to accommodate itself to a more industrial South. It certainly will be unlikely that southern cities like Memphis, Birmingham, Atlanta, New Orleans, and Louisville will allow themselves to be taxed indefinitely to subsidize an outworn system of rural local government.

There are nearly fifteen hundred counties in the fifteen southern states. County offices are the centers of the power of the county seat elite. Like all governing classes there is a tendency for them to become hereditary with office falling repeatedly in one family or for long terms of tenure in the hands of the same man. As Mosca long since pointed out:

> .... In the first place, all ruling classes tend to become hereditary in fact if not in law. All political forces seems to possess a quality that in physics used to be called the force of inertia. They have a tendency, that is, to remain at the point and in the state in which they find themselves.[7]

Such is the ironical consequence of Jacksonian Democracy with its election of all local officials! It is only a question of time until the urban South bursts the fetters of county seat feudal institutions and becomes free. The organization of labor is almost essential to this development. It is hence possible that we may have a great deal of labor and farmer conflict, though the interests of the two are fundamentally alike in their need for greater production and mutual exchange of their products.

The standards of urban living and technological working will demand the retraining of hundreds of thousands, if not millions of rural dwellers. Not only must skills be improved but attitudes must be modified. City living demands cooperative frames of mind not necessary to rural life. Mankind, not only in the South, but everywhere, must consciously and deliberately plan to eradicate hatred, fundamentally based upon fear and insecurity, or mankind will disappear from the earth. The negative attitude of tolerance is not enough at the pace modern technology has set. We must build positively or expect our suspicions and frustrations to destroy us. The atomic environment must breed sufficient good will to maintain our institutions or the end is inevitable.

The pattern for adult education has long been set. Thomas Jefferson and John Quincy Adams, Virginian and Puritan alike, believed in science.[8] Whether they foresaw that the only freedom for mankind from the curse of "original sin" was to enslave machines to escape enslaving human beings, I do not know. Both believed in the development of reason and in educating the masses of men. During the dread civil conflict, the first act of substantial federal aid to higher education was started. It was to be education in agriculture and mechanics, to develop science, if you will.[9] The institution of which you are a part owes its existence, in no small measure, to the Morrill Act. The progress which has been made has been slow but significant. How different the farming in the fourth decade of the twentieth century from that of 1900! If it is possible for government to foster science in agriculture, in the making of two blades of grass to grow where only one grew before, then is it not possible to improve the quality of human living by the same process of demonstration and subsidized consent? Is it not possible to demonstrate how workers and managers may more profitably live together? Is it not possible to demonstrate what are good racial relations? Certainly in this way lies the road to freedom. The man who is a victim of fears, real or illusory, is neither free nor happy. The property owner who has to barricade himself against his slaves, or against his free workers, is not free any more than the slave who fears his master's lash or the laborer who dreads his employer's displeasure.

In reality, there is no solution to the farmer's problem of surplus except full employment, at high real wages, of all workers. He must have this assurance of a market before he is free to produce an abundance. When this security comes to him he will be able to take care of his soil, to rid himself of the haunting fear of glutted markets and price depressing surpluses. Rid of these fears the farmer, no less than the manager and the laborer, will once more be a free man. The disintegrating influence of pressure politics will be relaxed when the defeating fears which generated the race for scarcity will be found no longer to exist. The fear of abundance has dominated American business, agriculture, and labor too long. The fear of man, mother of the hatred of man, must disappear in the presence of potential plenty. The economic problems of the South, of the nation, and of the world will never have any prospect of solution until they are approached from the consumer's point of view of abundance rather than the producer's conceptions of coercive scarcity.

Does all of this mean the destruction of the southern tradition? I think not. Traditions are to societies what habits are to individuals. Traditions are customary ways of doing things, useful because we can do more without reasoning out the details repeatedly. There were good reasons for the formation of the traditions or the habits but usually the reasons have been forgotten. Traditions and habits need to be discarded when they are no longer useful. However, traditions can frequently be modified to serve new purposes as well as the outmoded ones. Hence, we need to examine the southern tradition to see if there are factors in it which may be helpful in the solution of present difficulties.

First of all, there is the southern tradition of creative statesmanship which comes to us from Washington, Jefferson, Madison, and Wilson. The public life is worthwhile and justifies the sacrifice of personal ambition or private gain for the sake of the general welfare. This view of life carries with it the conception of taking the long-range, the over-all view of political problems, rather than the immediate and short-range outlook. Surely if Jefferson's, Washington's, or, for that matter, Clay's long-range view of slavery had been general, gradual emancipation might have been possible and the transition from a feudal to a capitalistic economy could have been made without violence. If the modern South will take the Jeffersonian view, I think it will be possible to inaugurate and carry out the change from the present sharecropper system to a more highly mechanized agriculture without violence and without too great a dislocation in the entire southern economy. As Jefferson put it in urging popular control of government:

> . . . . Do not be frightened into their [true principles] surrender by the alarms of the timid, or the croakings of wealth against the ascendancy of the people. . . . . The true foundation of republican government is the equal right of every citizen, in his person and property, and in their management. Try by this, as a tally, every provision of our constitution, and see if it hangs directly on the will of the people. . . . .
> . . . . But I know also that laws and institutions must go hand in hand with the progress of the human mind. As that becomes more developed, more enlightened, as new discoveries are made, new truths disclosed, and manners and opinions change with the change of circumstances, institutions must advance also, and keep pace with the times. We might as well require a man to wear still the coat which fitted him when a boy, as civilized society to remain ever under the regimen of their barbarous ancestors.[10]

Brooks Adams has suggested that George Washington's ultimate aim was the construction of federal highways and canals which would link North and South, East and West together and thereby avoid civil war.[11] His was the long-range view. We need this national, yes, international, long-range view in the future of southern politics. This is the true Jeffersonian democracy; that view has no room for a narrow provincial conception which, in the guise of states' rights, looks backward only. Jefferson had his sights fixed on the distant goal; there was never any danger of his turning to a pillar of political salt because he was looking backward. It is really too bad that the dead cannot protect themselves from libels on their good names!

In the next place, the South has a tradition of good or gentle breeding and warm hospitality. These virtues are worthy ones. The test of good breeding, of true social courtesy, is not how we treat our social superiors or equals, but how we behave to our social inferiors. The gentleman will never be anything but kind and courteous to those who are poor, sick, ignorant, or unfortunate. He never reminds another of his social inferiority—to do so is to reveal his own lack of gentility, his coarseness and ill breeding. The inculcation of this southern traditional ideal can do much to soften the relations between the races. The gentleman is fair and honorable in his dealings with all. One cannot imagine Robert E. Lee, for example, withholding from a poor Negro the prize he had legitimately won in a lottery. Once more we have the example of Jefferson who, writing of a talented free Negro citizen observed:

> I shall be delighted to see these instances of moral eminence so multiplied as to prove that the want of talents observed in them is merely the effect of their degraded condition, and not proceeding from any difference in the structure of the parts on which intellect depends.[12]

The traditional respect for genuine honor cannot be overemphasized. Certainly the honor system among students as inaugurated at the University of Virginia was an integral part of Jefferson's conception of the role of a democratic elite. It is to be remembered that Jefferson wanted a highly selective school system to enable the best, the most promising young men, "the geniuses out of the rubbish," as he expressed it, to attend his university. These young men were to be trained in philosophy and the sciences, but, most significant of all, they were to be disciplined in self-government. If man cannot govern himself, he cannot govern others; this is the essence of the Jeffersonian spirit.[13] Self-restraint is certainly the spiritual motif of Jefferson's governing class, not self-indulgence. Self-regulation, self-control, the sovereignty of reason, is the foundation of a governing class worthy of the name. The fulfillment of Jefferson's conception of the role of a state university in educating a worthy governing class can be measured by the success or failure of honor systems on the campuses of southern universities and colleges. If the people of a state cannot expect the finest products of their highest schools and educational institutions not to be cheats, then the prospects for the future of southern politics is dark, indeed.

Of course, it may be written of a new governing class, produced by our universities, as Mosca has written, with European universities in mind:

> The intelligence and the psychology of a man of the lower middle class, who has managed to win a university degree or even a secondary school diploma, are almost always closer to those of a millionaire than to those of a workingman, though from an economic standpoint a man of the lower middle class stands closer to the workingman than he does to the millionaire. All that is a result of progress in culture, in what Italians call "civility," whereby those who devote themselves to intellectual pursuits, and sometimes to the refinements of leisure, necessarily become more and more differentiated from the social strata that are devoted exclusively to manual pursuits and are fitted for no other.[14]

A new, bolder governing class must develop in the South. Its vision must reach beyond the courthouse in the county seat, yes even beyond the statehouse and the dome of the national capitol to the proposed new world capitol on Manhattan. Such statesmen are not beyond precedent in the South. One of them left the South, but within southern tradition, pleaded for world unity and for a League of Nations to save the world from the disaster of a second world war. A second southern statesman, born in the hills of Tennessee, preserved the ideals of Woodrow Wilson in his heart, and over a long period of time won universal respect as a symbol of world order, world peace and universal brotherhood. I speak, of course, of Cordell Hull.

The paradox of the South is that it has been, at once, the most provincial and the most international of our sections. The paradox must pass, for provincialism must yield to the larger order. The accomplishments of Oak Ridge, Tennessee, have forever banished the picture of Dayton, Tennessee. Science and statesmanship must go hand in hand if either is to survive. The art, or science, of statesmanship must win anew its right to a high place in the hierarchy of professions. No longer must the term "politician" be one of reproach to be used in the same breath with "gangster" and "racketeer." Mothers must want their boys to be politicians as much as they now want them to be lawyers, doctors, engineers, and certainly more than insurance or bond salesmen. Statesmanship must be recognized as the art of reconciling conflicting groups so that policies may be determined and personnel selected without violence. Most important of all, social institutions must accommodate themselves to technological change without violence, for the technique of violence is now so highly developed that man himself can no longer utilize it without destroying the society he expects to alter. In other words, statesmen must be social engineers who guide, direct, and control social evolution. They must rise above prejudice and bias even as Hugo Black is doing on the United States Supreme Court today.

Reconstruction in the South was a failure. At last we are in a position to start a conscious and intelligent policy of reconstruction. The Tennessee Valley Authority is a move toward genuine reconstruction, belated it is true, but an effort to create new wealth, and a positive step in developing natural resources. In another respect, it was not self-generated but was imposed from the outside. It may have been acquiesced in at the grass roots but it was not created there, certainly not at southern grass roots. The South must not expect social regeneration from the federal government; it must initiate and aggressively want a reconstruction in its human values.

It is ironic that the section which boasts of itself as the most Protestant part of America should do so little for the genuine dignity of the individual, for nowhere are so many individuals humiliated so often by so many. A creative politics must start not only with the dignity of the individual but it must found itself upon the dignity and worth of productive labor. The old invidious distinction between manual and nonmanual labor must be buried. Because it has more people, because it prides itself upon individualism, there must be a recognition of human independence—independence of party, custom, and convention. Neither the coercive power of violence nor the inertia of custom nor the force of economic sanction must be used against the nonconformist. Without free men there can be no free enterprise or free labor. The Thirteenth Amendment must at last be accepted in fact, in action, and in spirit. Laws must be intended to develop independence of spirit in all men, the worker no less than the manager. In this fashion we may have a creative future in southern politics. In this kind of future we may find more Jeffersons and fewer Byrds, more Hulls and fewer Bilbos, more Wilsons and fewer Huey Longs.

The politics of the future must be the organization of affection, not the organization of hatreds. A new two-party system will arise in the future as in the past, for as Jefferson wrote Lafayette, "The parties of Whig and Tory are those of nature. They exist in all countries. . . . . The sickly, weakly, timid man fears the people, and is a Tory by nature. The healthy, strong and bold, cherishes them, and is formed a Whig by nature."[15]

It is a commonplace to say we are at one of the great crossroads of human history. There is no turning back. Democracy is either a creative force or is doomed. Will it be said of us as Hegel once wrote "Minerva's owl begins its flight only in the gathering dusk"? Shall we see the real

A CREATIVE FUTURE? 93

nature of democracy, as Plato and Aristotle saw the real nature of the Greek city-state, when the twilight has already set in? Political democracy is confronted by a great challenge which calls itself social democracy. In the Soviet Union racial intolerance has been crushed, by violence it is true, and, therefore perhaps impermanently, but cultural autonomy has been achieved. Political democracy as we understand it does not exist in the Soviet Union, but recurring cycles of plenty and scarcity have been controlled, although at too high a price. We cannot offset the ideology of "social" democracy by calling it bad names, or by sending bayonets to hungry people threatened by an ideology of social equality. Food, clothing, and shelter produced by an enterprise, really free, free of monopoly as well as of government control, is the best answer. The South has its opportunity to set a mighty example to the world. It can bring to bear the Jeffersonian tradition, the real and authentic tradition of the South, to help solve the problems of contemporary man. Thus every southern state university can say with Jefferson:

"This institution of my native state .... will be based on the illimitable freedom of the human mind to explore and to expose every subject susceptible of its contemplation."[16]

The governing class of the new South will need to be taught by a group of scholars believing in this ideal, who themselves are willing to be bold and courageous and who are able to inculcate this courage and boldness in their students. Both students and teachers will need to follow the lead of Mr. Justice Holmes and climb the lonely heights of thought, for:

> Only when you have worked alone—when you have felt around you a black gulf of solitude more isolating than that which surrounds the dying man, and in hope and in despair have trusted to your own unshaken will—then only will you have achieved. Thus only can you gain the secret isolated joy of the thinker, who knows that, a hundred years after he is dead and forgotten, men who never heard of him will be moving to the

measure of his thought—the subtile rapture of a postponed power, which the world knows not because it has no external trappings, but which to his prophetic vision is more real than that which commands an army.[17]

REFERENCES

LECTURE I, PAGE 1 TO PAGE 15

1. See the excellent discussion in E. E. Schattschneider, *Party Government* (New York: Farrar and Rinehart, Inc., 1942), pp. 65-98.

2. George Burton Adams, *Civilization During the Middle Ages, Especially in Relation to Modern Civilization* (New York: Charles Scribner's Sons, 1922), pp. 195-6.

3. Aristotle, *A Treatise on Government* (Everyman's Library; New York: E. P. Dutton, 1912), pp. 6-7.

4. It is not contended that the plantation was exclusively feudal, for the plantation became a type of exploitative and capitalistic agriculture. For full treatment, see L. C. Gray and Esther K. Thompson, *History of Agriculture in the Southern United States to 1860* (Washington: Carnegie Institute of Washington, 1933), two volumes.

5. Henry Adams, *The Education of Henry Adams* (New York: The Modern Library, 1931), pp. 57-8.

6. Thorstein Veblen, *Theory of the Leisure Class* (New York: Vanguard Press, 1926).

7. Clement Eaton, *Freedom of Thought in the Old South* (Durham: Duke University, 1940), p. 5.

8. *Public Opinion* (New York: The Macmillan Company, 1922), chap. 1.

9. Eaton, *op. cit.*, p. 5.

10. For a discussion of the hill people see the fine volume of H. C. Nixon, *Lower Piedmont Country* (New York: Duell, Sloan, and Pierce, 1946), especially chapter 14.

11. In general, A. C. Cole, *The Whig Party in the South* (Washington: American Historical Association, 1913). For a more specialized treatment, J. B. Shannon's unpublished manuscript, "Henry Clay as a Political Leader," 1934.

12. James Truslow Adams, *America's Tragedy* (New York: Charles Scribner's Sons, 1934), pp. 150-8. See also, R. S. Cotterill, *The Old South* (Glendale, California: Arthur H. Clark Company, 1936), pp. 317-19.

REFERENCES

13. Nathaniel S. Shaler, *Kentucky* (New York: Houghton, 1884), pp. 232-3.
14. E. Merton Coulter, *The Civil War and Readjustment in Kentucky* (Chapel Hill: The University of North Carolina Press, 1926), p. 53.
15. Richard N. Current, *Old Thad Stevens* (Madison: The University of Wisconsin Press, 1942), pp. 226-9.
16. C. Vann Woodward, *Tom Watson: Agrarian Rebel* (New York: The Macmillan Company, 1938), especially chapter XIII.
17. *Bailey* v. *Alabama*, 219 U. S. 219 (1911). Opinion of Mr. Justice Hughes.
18. There is little or no printed material on the subject. This discussion is based on the author's independent investigation contained in an unprinted manuscript, "Tenancy in the Big Bend of the Tennessee River: A Summary," Knoxville, 1938.
19. *Evans* v. *State*, 83 So. 167, 168 (1919).
20. *Chambers* v. *Baldwin*, 15 S. W. 57 (1891); *Boulier et al.* v. *Macauley*, 15 S. W. 60 (1891).
21. Francis Barnes Sayre, "Inducing Breach of Contract," *Harvard Law Review*, 663-703 (1922-23).

LECTURE II, PAGE 16 TO PAGE 37

1. Walter J. Shepard, "Theory of the Nature of Suffrage," *Proceedings of the American Political Science Association*, VII (1913), 107-36.
2. Letter of May 27, 1867. Edward L. Pierce, *Memoirs and Letters of Charles Sumner*. (Boston: Roberts Brothers, 1893), IV, 319.
3. *Washington* v. *State*, 75 Ala. 582, 584 (1884).
4. Quoted in Peter H. Odegard and E. Allen Helms, *American Politics* (Rev. Ed.; New York: Harper and Brothers, 1947), p. 362.
5. Rousseau, *Social Contract* (Everyman's Library; New York: E. P. Dutton, 1913), pp. 25, 90-2.

6. J. S. Mill, *Utilitarianism, Liberty, Representative Government* (Everyman's Library; New York: E. P. Dutton, 1910), pp. 278-9.

7. Woodward, *op. cit.*

8. Quoted in Paul Lewinson, *Race, Class, and Party* (New York: Oxford University Press, 1932), p. 38.

9. John D. Hicks, *The Populist Revolt* (Minneapolis: The University of Minnesota Press, 1931), p. 263.

10. (Auburn, Ala.: Auburn Printing Company, 1927), p. 147. Italics supplied by the author.

11. Hicks, *op. cit.*, pp. 391-3.

12. Dunbar Rowland, *History of Mississippi*, (Second ed.; Jackson: Mississippi Department of Archives and History, 1925), II, 607.

13. *Ibid.*, II, 252.

14. *Ibid.*, II, 253.

15. *Ratliff*, Sheriff, v. *Beale*, 74 Mississippi 247; 20 So. 865, 868 (1896).

16. *Ratliff*, Sheriff, v. *Beale*, 74 Mississippi 247; 20 So. 865, 869.

17. *Ratliff*, Sheriff, v. *Beale*, 74 Mississippi 247; 20 So. 865, 869.

18. *Journal of the Proceedings of the Convention of Delegates Elected by the People of Tennessee to Amend, Revise, or Form and Make a New Constitution for the State* (Nashville: Jones, Purvis, and Co., 1870), pp. 179-81.

19. "Tenancy in the Big Bend of the Tennessee River," *op. cit.*, p. 72.

20. Ralph C. McDanel, *The Virginia Constitutional Convention of 1901-1902* (Baltimore: Johns Hopkins University Studies, 1928), p. 58.

21. *Nixon* v. *Herndon et al.*, 273 U. S. 536 (1927).

22. *Newberry et al.* v. *U. S.*, 256 U. S. 232 (1921).

23. *Nixon* v. *Condon*, 286 U. S. 73 (1932).

24. *Grovey* v. *Townsend*, 295 U. S. 45 (1935).

25. *Smith* v. *Allwright*, 321 U. S. 649 (1944).

REFERENCES

26. *Elmore* v. *Rice et al.*, 72 Fed. Supp. 516 (1947).
27. *Breedlove* v. *Suttles*, 302 U. S. 277 (1937).
28. *United States* v. *Classic*, 313 U. S. 299 (1940).
29. Italics supplied by the author.
30. *United States* v. *Classic*, 313 U. S. 299, 314.
31. *United States* v. *Classic*, 313 U. S. 299, 315.
32. *United States* v. *Classic*, 313 U. S. 299, 319.
33. *United States* v. *Classic*, 313 U. S. 299, 330.
34. *United States* v. *Classic*, 313 U. S. 299, 329.
35. *Senate Report No. 1662*, 77th Congress, 2nd Session, reprinted in *Hearings before the Committee of the Judiciary of the United States Senate*, 78th Congress, 1st Session (Washington: United States Government Printing Office, 1942), pp. 5-6.
36. For an excellent review of the legal aspects, see Joseph E. Kallenbach, "Constitutional Aspects of Federal Anti-Poll Tax Legislation," in 45 *Michigan Law Review*, 717-32 (1947).

LECTURE III, PAGE 38 TO PAGE 53

1. Harold D. Lasswell, *Politics; Who Gets What, When, How* (New York & London: Whittlesey House, McGraw-Hill Book Company, 1936), p. 3.
2. Gaetano Mosca, *The Ruling Class* (New York: McGraw-Hill Book Company, 1939), p. 50.
3. Eaton, *op. cit.*, p. 48.
4. Henry Adams, *op. cit.*, pp. 237-8.
5. See Matthew Josephson, *The Robber Barons* (New York: Harcourt, Brace & Company, 1934).
6. Robert Somers, *The Southern States Since the War 1870-1* (London and New York: The Macmillan Company, 1871), p. 116.
7. *Ibid.*, p. 119.
8. Clark, *op. cit.*, pp. 28-9.
9. Brooks Adams, *The Theory of Social Revolutions* (New York: The Macmillan Company, 1913), pp. 215-16.

LECTURE IV, PAGE 54 TO PAGE 72

1. Portions of this lecture were published in *Vital Speeches*, XIII (August 15, 1947), 645-50.

2. William Allen White to Henry Wallace, August, 1944; quoted in Russell Lord, *The Wallaces of Iowa* (Boston: Houghton Mifflin & Co., 1947), p. 517.

3. See, in general, Charles A. Beard, *American Party Battle* (New York: Workers Education Bulletin, 1928).

4. Woodward, *op. cit.*, *passim*.

5. A careful reading of Bryan's "Cross of Gold" speech will disclose the groups to whose interests the great orator was appealing.

6. The nature of this contest is very effectively shown in *The Autobiography of William Allen White* (New York: The Macmillan Company, 1946), pp. 462-8.

7. Apparently Mr. Roosevelt himself was responsible for this bargain. See Edward J. Flynn, *You're the Boss* (New York: Viking Press, 1947), p. 104.

8. See J. B. Shannon, "Presidential Politics in the South," *Journal of Politics*, I (February, 1939), 297.

9. For example, the late Senator Pat Harrison of Mississippi opposed Roosevelt's first nomination, apparently for reasons of big business interest. Flynn, *op. cit.*, pp. 100-101.

10. Jones had been "an extremely active candidate" for the vice-presidential nomination in 1940. *Ibid.*, p. 157. For a discussion of the Jones-Wallace feud, see Russell Lord, *op. cit.*, pp. 496-514.

11. According to Flynn, Roosevelt himself selected Truman to succeed Wallace. Flynn, *op. cit.*, pp. 180-1.

12. Henry Adams, *op. cit.*, p. 7.

13. "Ilya Ehrenburg's America," *Harper's Magazine*, 193 (December, 1946), 570-1.

14. William Allen White, *A Puritan in Babylon* (New York: The Macmillan Company, 1938), pp. 260-1.

15. Sherman E. Johnson, "Farm Science and Citizens," in *Science in Farming: The Yearbook of Agriculture, 1943–1947* (Washington: United States Government Printing Office, 1947), p. 922.

16. See Frank J. Welch and D. Gray Miley, *Mechanization of the Cotton Harvest*, Bulletin 420, Mississippi State College, June, 1945.

17. George C. Stoney, "No Room in Green Pastures," *Survey Graphic*, XXX, No. 1 (1941) 16.

18. Theodore H. White, "The Battle of Athens, Tennessee," *Harper's Magazine*, 194 (January, 1947), 52-61.

19. Report of the Committee on Education and Labor, *Violations of Free Speech and Rights of Labor*, Report 6, Part 2 (Washington: United States Government Printing Office, 1939).

20. (3rd ed.; New York: Alfred A. Knopf, 1921), pp. 30-1.

21. Sigmund Neumann, *Permanent Revolution* (New York: Harper and Brothers, 1942).

22. Peter Drucker, *The Future of Industrial Man* (Toronto: Longmans, Green, and Co., 1942).

23. John Fischer, "The Lost Liberals," *Harper's Magazine*, 194 (May, 1947), 391.

LECTURE V, PAGE 73 TO PAGE 94

1. *Mark Twain's Autobiography* (New York and London: Harper and Brothers, 1924), II, 7.

2. *Journal of Proceedings of Tennessee Constitutional Convention, op. cit.*, pp. 97-8.

3. Gamaliel Bradford, *Lee The American* (Boston: Houghton Mifflin Company, 1912), p. 249.

4. Wallas, *op. cit.*, pp. 154-5.

5. John Nicolay and John Hay, *The Complete Works of Abraham Lincoln* (New and enlarged edition, Harrogate, Tenn.: Lincoln Memorial University, 1894), V, 251-2.

6. Mill, *op. cit.*, pp. 193-5.

7. Mosca, *op. cit.*, p. 61.

8. Henry Adams, *Degradation of the Democratic Dogma* (New York: The Macmillan Company, 1920), pp. 65-75.

9. For a general discussion of the significance of this legislation, see John M. Gaus and L. O. Wolcott, *Public Administration and the United States Department of Agriculture* (Chicago: Public Administration Service, 1940), pp. 11-12.

10. Bernard Mayo, *Jefferson Himself* (Boston: Houghton Mifflin Company, 1942), pp. 323-4.

11. Brooks Adams' introduction to Henry Adams, *Degradation of the Democratic Dogma*, *op. cit.*, pp. 13-18.

12. Jefferson to Condorcet, August 30, 1791. Quoted in Adrienne Koch, *The Philosophy of Thomas Jefferson* (New York: Columbia University Press, 1943), pp. 118-19.

13. First inaugural address, "Sometimes it is said that man cannot be trusted with the government of himself. Can he, then, be trusted with the government of others?" Quoted in Mayo, *op. cit.*, p. 222.

14. Mosca, *op. cit.*, p. 471.

15. Koch, *op. cit.*, p. 123.

16. Mayo, *op. cit.*, p. 327.

17. Oliver Wendell Holmes, *Collected Legal Papers* (Boston: Little, Brown and Company, 1920), p. 32.

This book has been set in Bodoni type by the McQuiddy Printing Company of Nashville, Tennessee.